something that is closer to ignition than commital—"not a backfire, but an explosion. And the fallout will be just great."

The Last Years Of The Church is a forceful, engrossing, analytic description of what's going on in today's churches. It explains what is meant by expressions like "underground church," and how the Church has related to the military, the moral climate, the race problem in America. It explains why fewer people attend services, why the shortage of spiritual leaders in the Church has become critical, and what the new generation is seeking that their churches have failed to provide.

Mr. Poling does not believe that the secular world alone has all the answers. There are still things that are holy and sacred, and there is still a need for religion and Church in modern times. And in these pages he speculates on the new shape of Christian involvement with society—the first years of the *new* Church.

PHOTO BY BLACKSTONE-SHELBURNE

David Poling was born in New Jersey in 1928, grew up in Texas, and went to Yale Divinity School. He served Presbyterian parishes in LeRoy, New York, Buffalo, and Bartlesville, Oklahoma, before becoming editor of *The Christian Herald* in 1964. He is now President of the *Christian Herald Association;* his articles on religion have appeared in national magazines such as *McCalls,* and *The Saturday Review;* his weekly newspaper column is syndicated in 600 papers; and he has appeared frequently on television and radio programs and lecture platforms.

The Last Years of the Church

The LAST YEARS of the CHURCH

David Poling

GARDEN CITY, NEW YORK

DOUBLEDAY & COMPANY, INC.

1969

Library of Congress Catalog Card Number 69–10954

Printed in the United States of America

The author is grateful to the following publishers for the use of copyrighted material:

Broadcasting for "Are you running with us, God?" from *Broadcasting Magazine,* November 21, 1966.

The Christian Century Foundation for material from "The Assassination from a Christological Perspective" by Donald E. Miller and Graydon F. Snyder, copyright 1964 Christian Century Foundation. Reprinted by permission from the April 1964 issue of *The Pulpit.*

Farrar, Straus & Giroux, Inc., for selections from *O the Chimneys,* reprinted with permission of Farrar, Straus & Giroux, Inc., from *O the Chimneys* by Nelly Sachs. Copyright © 1967 by Farrar, Straus & Giroux, Inc.

The General Commission on Chaplains and Armed Forces Personnel for material from "The Men Who Fly" by Chaplain Ormonde S. Brown, reprinted with permission from *The Chaplain,* March–April 1968.

here and now for material from "Renewal of the Church is for the Birds" by Gordon Gregg, from *here and now, a christian journal of opinion,* Dayton, Ohio, June 1967.

Longmans, Green & Co. Limited for material from *The Vision of God* by K. E. Kirk.

The Newspaper Enterprise Association, Inc., 7 East 43rd Street, New York, New York, for exerpts used in Chapters 2, 3, and 6 that have appeared in the author's column.

St. Anthony Messenger, 1615 Republic Street, Cincinnati, Ohio, for material from "Dynamic Duo," August 1966.

United Church Press for material from *A Man's Faith* by Wilfred T. Grenfell, M.D. The Pilgrim Press, 1908.

The Wall Street Journal for excerpts from "Negro Youth Returns to College by Stirring Prudential's Sympathy," *The Wall Street Journal,* March 20, 1968.

Contents

Introduction

We are witnessing the last years of the church. . . . The final days of the church as we have known it during our lifetime. Such a statement seems to indicate that one's attitude is reeking with some kind of anti-Christian poison. That is not the case. I trust that this book will show where I stand concerning the Christian faith as well as my commitment to it. And what I believe about the church and what has happened to it.

These are the last years of the church. But one does not make such a pronouncement without a lengthy period of observation and analysis. And with all of your loyalties and emotional involvements, your years of constant attention and anxiety, you don't just sit down some afternoon and say, "Well, I guess it's all over and we ought to let the people waiting know it." It hasn't happened that way. And the church isn't alone.

In fact, you could say these are the last years of the . . . educational system, or city hall, or the medical profession. For everywhere about us the old structures of authority and discipline are under siege. From one culture to another every establishment and seat of power now looks out upon a city square where the little people are gathering and murmuring. Some already have started to shake their umbrellas and canes in the air. Demonstrations accompany decline.

So teachers picket their own schools while students mill about on playgrounds. And doctors boycott their patients and priests circle city governments with banners and petitions. It's a tough hour for mayors, bishops, and building inspectors. Every human arrangement is under question, if not attack, and the church has not been spared—nor should it be!

If the church watchers had kept a journal or diary of the early warning signs of decline in ecclesiastical control, they might have first noted the slip in seminary enrollment. What has become an alarming drop in recent years began a decade ago with just a faint decrease from one year to the next.

So now seminaries are closing, and some rushing to last-gasp mergers and a few consolidating with universities that can support them in their declining years. The faultfinders will accuse the traditional church for its flimsy evangelism or lackluster recruiting efforts. Others sigh and credit the Peace Corps with a better selling job—or a more meaningful encounter with life. Either way, the decline of leadership means an extensive weakening of the church, already short on staff and swinging ideas.

There are no readily available statistics on Protestant ministers leaving their churches, though we know that there are many such dropouts. And we know that a thousand priests "officially" left the Catholic Church in 1967 alone. Add or subtract these one thousand, and you realize that things are beginning to surface in a menacing way for the traditionalists who believe it can't happen here. (The company didn't want to make any noise about it or cause any embarrassment to the church fathers, but nearly a hundred clergymen applied to Xerox Corp. last year for management and sales positions, a border crossing for many who wished to enter secular employment.)

The last years of the church are seen not only in the separations that have come from losing a Charles Davis in England, surely one of the top Roman Catholic scholars in the British Isles, but in the men and women who will not seek ordination or church appointments.

I was struck forcefully by this fact when I read Michael Novak's brilliant account of Vatican II, entitled *The Open Church.*

> To the man of good will the Catholic Church is not attractive . . . it is very difficult to see how one could ever find one's way into the faith. Imagine looking around: building fund campaigns; Masses on television; billboards about the family that prays together; a public obsession with sexual morality, which sounds Manichean rather than Christian; a legalistic morality; the lack of creativity; the public lack of candor; the defensiveness; the bored faces of ministers at the altar; the listlessness of the people; the misleadingly expressed doctrines; the censoring of books.

Raised in the religious community, prepared for ordination in a seminary in Rome, Novak turned to the university instead of the cathedral for his Christian fulfillment. The disillusionment of ministers and the general disarray in their ranks is just as complete in the Protestant churches, though not so obvious because of the many divisions and denominations.

Before he died in 1967, the very liberal Dutch Roman Catholic Bishop William M. Bekkers said:

> The priest began as a layman. God tapped him on the shoulder and led him through busy streets along the way that he must follow for the rest of his life. He walks along with everyone else using the street, but his path always ends in the church building.

And that is the heart of the problem. The Christian faith cannot and will not be limited, restricted, or defined by a building, museum, or shrine. The decline of the church may be another illustration of the way that the Christian gospel liberates men and society from the forms and crusts that would restrict and distort lives.

On the harsh economic side of things the church may be too expensive and costly to maintain. Some new living accommodations are prescribed. The cities are groaning and in some places gasping under the free tax ride that the "non-profits" enjoy. George Orwell may have been frightfully close when he said:

> The Christian Churches would probably not survive on their own merits if their economic basis were destroyed.

I have been in city churches where the choir outnumbered the audience. The people were gone, out of touch, unconcerned, but the building goes marching on with its quarterly dividends. Shall we mourn the last years of a church that looks out upon the world with the appearance of a Federal Reserve Branch, staffed by uniformed guards who suspiciously peer at humanity from the safety of stained glass that is bulletproof, foolproof, and compassion-proof!

These are the last years of the church when you can live in New York City for four years and never have a visitor or caller or luncheon guest or commuter mention or quote or praise or criticize a preacher! When pastors or congregations or religious societies are mentioned only on the church page—in paid advertisements—you know that something has set in, and it is not the ascendancy of a church we have always known.

So we'll struggle with this issue and speculate on the new shape of Christian involvement as the old forms sigh and expire. For we live in a time when the whole world is asking not about the inspiration of the scriptures but about the implementation of the gospel. We are surrounded with a new young generation that is bursting to ask the moral question, to hear the piercing word of truth and challenge, to feel the pounding heart of compassion and concern that has forever been the hallmark of the Christian.

And never has there been such an urgency to ask the tough, blunt questions of a society and people that claims all the answers.

It may be that the new Christian fellowship will have

communion without the table, wine without the cup, bread without the blessing. Already we are hearing the gospel without the cathedral. Or do you still believe that the path of Christ always leads to the church door?

The last years of the church! Not meant in derision or geriatric pity. Not in the smug assurance of a fraternity smoker or with the papal judgments of a *Playboy* editorial.

But the Last Years of the Church as a prelude to something which is closer to ignition than committal. Not a backfire, but an explosion. And the fallout will be just great.

For Ann my wife

my favorite theologian

ACKNOWLEDGMENTS

The author is indebted to:

Kenneth L. Wilson, Editor of *Christian Herald*, for his dialogue on the Christian faith—in editorial offices, commuter trains, and in Swedish cinema.

Boyd Lewis, Robert Metz, Robert Cochnar of the Newspaper Enterprise Association for their aid, comfort and criticism in the development of a much wider ministry than I ever dreamed.

Mrs. William L. Barrett for her thoughtful diligence in the preparation of this manuscript.

«I»

The Church and Change

American citizens are used to seeing the pictures of large shipments of wheat being unloaded on the wharfs of Calcutta or Bombay. On the side of the sacks, barrels, and cartons, in bold letters, is stamped: *Aid from the United States*. It is not fair to criticize the public-relations effect of this good work—except to say that a lot of people do not read English! It is positive help to those in difficult straits. Also it is official.

For countless generations, people within the Christian church have expected to receive some kind of credit for the good works they have performed. I don't say that cynically or sarcastically, but matter-of-factly. They have paid the freight and they have a vital interest in the project, be it a hospital in New Mexico, a college in Puerto Rico, a clinic in Lebanon. Over the years, denominational promotion managers, mission-board personnel, local pastors—all involved in necessary fund raising—have had motion pictures, Kodachrome slides, pamphlets, study guides, guest speakers to remind, inspire, and exhort the faithful to works of mercy.

The Style of the Secular Saint

The result has been impressive. Billions of dollars have been subscribed for the hundreds of church colleges, the thousands of hospitals and training schools, the dozens of seminaries, and the millions of people who have had an enormous amount of assistance and care around the globe. Christian outreach has been a dynamic force beyond all national borders, clans, and governments. However, we may be seeing a new turn of emphasis, a new thrust of concern in the style of the secular saint. Like those committed to the work of Jesus Christ, he cares for others. The sick, the hungry, the prisoner, the outcast—all are in the focus of his love and concern.

But be sure of the difference. His good works, public action, personal involvement have no ecclesiastical watermark, no stamp on the wheat sack, no sign on the front lawn that this is sponsored by the United Presbyterian Church. The secular saint may not make the sign of the Cross as the boats leave the harbor nor voice a declaration of faith as he suits up. But you can count on him. You can recognize him. You can meet him in action.

In the City

When you join the commuting scene, you develop consistent patterns of daily travel. Arrival and departure fit a tight schedule. I get so I sit almost in the same seat of the same car—reading the same paper and glaring at the same smokers who pollute the air in our non-smoker!

Month by month, coming out of Grand Central, hiking three blocks south to your office, you get so you could do it blindfolded. Coming out of the office in the evening, you retrace your steps, passing the high-rise office buildings, the Park Avenue line-up of Cadillacs waiting for the captains of industry, and then re-entry into your train.

Your mind absorbs many things visually. You realize, for instance, that the line-up of chauffeured cars is almost always the same. Certain drivers always seem to stand and visit outside their limousines, others are always behind the wheel, reading or staring into the early evening traffic. So with the men they whisk away. Always busy, well-groomed, with a brisk, confident big-deal pace—off to some sprawling estate in Long Island or Westchester or maybe living in town in high-rise happiness. No one tells you this. You just mentally record the scene, day after day, season after season, homburg after cashmere coat and imported shoes.

Then one evening you turn the corner and there on the sidewalk is one of your big-business princes crouching over a man. In a flash you can see that the one he holds has tripped, fallen, or fainted. His face is bruised. He makes gagging, choking, strangling noises in his throat. Then you also realize that the man in the silk suit and imported shoes and tailored shirt has put his linen handkerchief into the victim's mouth so he will not swallow his tongue. Emotion creeps over your midtown composure as you watch this corporation president wipe the victim's face, loosen his tie, and look up to see if his chauffeur has been able to flag a patrol car or ambulance.

The two had never met before. Their clothes, their work, their wallets had assigned them to different locations of New York. Yet, in this sudden tragic encounter, I observed much about a man I have never met, who operated with split-second compassion. He will never be blessed or burdened by churchly endorsement, a denominational publication cover, religious "man of the year," but he showed me the style of the secular saint, and I believe, made glad the heart of God.

The point is this: we are moving into the time about which Dietrich Bonhoeffer spoke, the Christian becoming the "man for others." This man for others may be a good distance from the regular definitions of the Christian institution. He may not be formally related to any church. The sacraments, as we currently observe them, may not find meaning in his life. The Lord's Supper and baptism may not be vital, essential events in his world. But he cares about people. His caring is spontaneous, forceful, and consistent with the way he sees the world. It has been my experience that the secular saint can be trusted in his life, he honors Christ with his deeds.

An Unheroic Period?

Reinhold Niebuhr once called this an unheroic period in the life of the church.

Did he mean that the age of adventure, the era of outreach which had fired thousands of young people to seek positions in Christian "foreign service" of the 1920s was no longer around?

Was he referring to the fact that blazing young liberals no longer went A.W.O.L. from seminary to walk the picket line of a Pullman strike or hand out leaflets at the gates of U. S. Steel . . . because they were nowhere to be found?

Did he consider the pacifists' protests of 1916 and 1936 to have been spent in the wars of this century, which swallowed their religious idealism when they saw Hitler's ovens and Eichmann's shipping charts?

Lastly, did Dr. Niebuhr mean that this age has no solid heroes because the issues can no longer be so firmly and fiercely drawn—that perhaps the church is implicated in the social malaise of our time and the gospel is only as true and lively as the caretakers make it, whether it be in parish, seminary, or cathedral precincts?

Indeed, one report on the ministry suggested, after studying the activities and daily round of the average clergyman, that he was really a "pastoral director" guiding the schedule of his people as they met for group worship, feeding, study, fun, and games. These may be necessary requirements of a church in the late twentieth century, but it hardly suggests candidates for martyrdom when an afternoon's project may be to mark off new diagonal lines for Sunday parking.

If the church has been slumbering, serving its people with program and purpose that are no more demanding than an annual antique show, Spring Fair, and Men's Sports Night (and how proud some people have been to tell their friends, "Why, this year we're going to have a colored baseball player speak!"), then it is little wonder that they have sought their heroes elsewhere. Lofty adventure is seen and experienced in the whole space program rocketing out of Cape Kennedy, with another astronaut in orbit, and another ten thousand youngsters wishing to be part of this celestial action.

Others, expressing well their need for adventure as keenly as their need for security, go all out in sports. Whether it be tennis or swimming or skating or skiing, countless thousands are enrolled in demanding, arduous routine to lower their time, extend their endurance, advance their standing, and reach out for the golden dream of stardom—which a few accomplish.

If some are denied participation through their own lack of talent or opportunity, they seize upon the stars of sports, stage, television, public life to enjoy success and achievement—even at a distance. I knew a couple in Buffalo, New York, that on almost every weekend would drive to Cleveland and back again to see their favorite Browns play. Snowstorms, pregnancy, Monday morning jobs were no deterrent to their addiction to follow a winning team. Their lives were nothing compared to the performance and drama delivered by their Sunday heroes.

It's nothing new, but I have lived in communities where youngsters seven, eight, nine, and older were up at dawn so they could swim a mile before their first classes. Hundreds of these bleary-eyed, running-nosed, infected-eared kids would climb in the water torture tank, stroke out the fifty, sixty laps and then hurry off to "secondary" education. Their parents would scan the schedule of swimming meets in the months ahead, carefully planning dates so that birthday parties, scout hikes, Sunday School classes, and dentist appointments would not conflict or cramp the child.

A few became champions. One or two were eclipsed next time around by some kid somewhere else who swam his fifty or sixty laps a little faster, whose mother planned the schedule a little better, and whose father found a sweeter carrot or snappier whip.

The Shapes of Heroic Action

Heroism, adventure, achievement, excitement, meaning—these are big words for a society surrounded by security, comfort, and entertainment. The youngster who is really alert can't hack it. Dad's business looks like a big bind, especially some of the corporate games people play. Getting a good education is a long operation and some drop out for reasons of pure ennui. They have the ability, the background, the skills, but not the drive or motivation to finish a course which has their whole life planned right down to the last family-room portraits.

Catching just enough of the mood which touches so many lives in mid-twentieth century, we should hardly marvel at the unique, instant success of the Peace Corps. It came as a viable alternative to the warfare society, to the American dream of Mustangs and drive-in movies. And a substantial, real live option to, yes, what the church had to offer—or the professions or Vietnam.

Commenting on the decline in seminary influence and enrollment, Malcolm Boyd observed that the Peace Corps was taking the top young people who normally would have found their way to church vocations in large numbers.

He went so far as to say that the Peace Corps just about buried the seminaries. I can't agree with that, since many may return to take up a career in the life of the church. What is clear is the fact that right now more than twenty thousand people are in training for the Peace Corps, representing people of all ages, backgrounds, and religious convictions. The very nature of the free and uncrowded theological positions of the Peace Corps has certainly been one of the appealing qualities for a generation that doesn't want to be boxed.

It might easily be claimed that there is plenty of heroic action around, considerable in the life of the Christian community, but it is just beginning to surface in forms and shapes that are very untraditional and unexpected.

The denominations that have been willing to establish and maintain urban ministries to inner-city neighborhoods have had plenty of reasons to cut and run when the Molotov cocktails were soaking up gasoline. They didn't because they had men and women tough enough to take on these asphalt jungles in the first place and love enough to stay when whole city blocks went up in flames. Harlem, East Harlem, Rochester, and Watts were in the center of the Burn, Baby, Burn movement. Yet each community knew the phonies from the soul brothers.

A reporter on the New York *Times* described the stark landscape of Watts with Westminster Neighborhood Center surrounded by charred rubble and smoldering foundations. But not Westminster with its Day Care Center for Youth, its writing classes, its counseling offices, and youth directors. St. Paul was right when he said the fire tested how we have built. In this instance, it revealed a new look of Christian witness, concern, and heroism. And when the squad cars leave and the firemen wrap up their hoses and the national guard stops patrolling, they are still there.

The Strategy of the Secular Saint

When the church no longer asks the hard, embarrassing questions about human relations, then the burden falls almost entirely upon those in the world beyond the sanctuary.

If justice is love in action, then we believe it to be a central theme in the Christian message. However, the church as institution, as "Christendom," has shown with regularity—even predictability—that it moves with lumbering difficulty to a point of leadership in society, content to be part of the scenery in place of making the scene.

In the life of Christ we see the steady build-up of

tension between Jesus and the religious establishment. Before we are too scathing about the usual villains—the Pharisees, the Sadducees, the Sanhedrin, and the Roman Government—let us keep vivid the thought that Jesus was called "rabbi," an honored, respected designation of the Pharisee school. That he perceived, studied, examined life with the historic support and inquiry of the Pharisaical school.

He was closer to the synagogue than the Temple. Yet his love and affection for the religious posture of the Jewish community—its rabbis, priests, and prophets, its law and Temple—made his criticism and exhortation all the more painful and cutting. To correct a stranger is one thing. To judge one's family and household is a supreme test of love and understanding. (We have the evidence from the synoptic Gospels that his family was among the first to suffer misunderstanding and distrust because of their son.)

When you review the biblical passages about the ministry of John the Baptist out in the sand traps beyond the Jordan, you realize that here was one who asked the brutal, unflinching questions about society. Compare his sign of redemption and salvation with that of any current popular evangelist, with or without lapel microphones, prime television exposure, and public-relations team. John the Baptist asked the hard, bludgeoning questions of moral righteousness.

He begged no authority from social position, claimed no platform of the Evangelical Association of Judea, asked for no pollster to tell the populace that he was the most popular figure since Jeremiah. His power and personality were fueled by the sense of the moral authority of God's judgment on a sick and wandering people. Beyond Jordan, he was a religious refugee. A secular saint beyond the holiness of the Temple, the observances of popular piety, and preparing the way for God's Annointed.

Repeat it:

> When the church no longer asks the hard, embarrassing questions about human relations, then the burden falls almost entirely upon those in the world beyond the sanctuary.

You can trace this theme from the beginning of biblical prophecy in the searing, burning men of God like Amos, Jeremiah, Hosea, Ezekiel, Isaiah, and John the Baptist.

At times, you think they will buckle under the pressure and bullying of a king, tyrant, friendly counsel, and inward doubt. Time and again they are ready to chicken out, lose their cool, be swallowed up in the moral consensus of the neighborhood group. But if anything stands out clearly in biblical drama, it is the raising up of men and women by God, to serve Him in justice, in the proclaiming of judgment, and in the certainty that this world was created for purpose and order.

Strangling the Word of God

You can take almost any period of human experience, and find the church (the religious community, the faithful worshipers, the standard-bearers, the fellowship of believers) in such comfortable acceptance of the activities of government, the goals of business, the pretensions of labor, the vulgarity of artistic endeavor, educational presumptions, that the Word of God is strangled in the syrup of belonging.

Over and over again God moved dramatically to work outside the church when its forms fossilized, its vitality turned to building and image, its organization became sacred, and the darting eyes of its leaders knew not the "true and lively Word."

Whether it be the period of Constantine, the era of the barbarian, the Reformation of Luther and Calvin, or the new struggle with world social and political revolution, the church has usually been late to perceive the unfolding developments and lost in any meaningful response to the requirements of the hour.

Those who are loyal to the church and respect its laws ask for more time, more understanding, more patience. Yet the world will not wait and computers spin and youngsters marry and wars increase. Science has not waited for the church to decide if it is moral or immoral, holy or profane.

The Church at Rome speaks haltingly about the joys and responsibilities of marriage, restrains discussions about new birth control methods, and millions will starve through ignorance and blind obedience. At a point when mankind enjoys extraordinary gains in family planning, the Church abdicates its moral leadership to the scientist and social strategist who counsels governments, community leaders, and midwives on the techniques of the preservation of life.

So the gap widens. Not just with the Church of Rome, but with all churches that have been winded by the pace of this century, confused by the demands and abilities of youth, warped by the old arguments of "Christian society," which no longer exists.

We may be alarmed with the credibility gap between the White House and my house, but it is not worse than the wardrobe gap of the Vatican princes or the Orthodox bishops. The robes and capes and hats and collars no longer spellbind a world culture that has a President's widow in a mini-skirt or a princess in a bikini.

A Change of Wardrobe

For decades men felt that the church, with its robes and high collars, lace and flowing garments, was quaint. Now it's queer and the more sensitive leaders, close to the pulse of the people and concerned for the lack of communication, have updated their hair styles and gone downtown for their wardrobes.

For many caring people in the ranks of Christian leadership, to serve God has been to leave the sacred quadrangle, the cloister, the cathedral setting, and be part of the secular scene. Across the world this is happening. Some stay in uniform. Others are willing to use the disguise and fashion of the world to secure their witness to Him who made life and calls us to creatively express it.

No more vivid illustration of this plunge into the secular world from the safety of the sacred could be found than in the person of Sister Jacqueline Grennan, president of Webster College outside of St. Louis, Missouri.

After a lengthy soul-sorting period, she announced that she wished to be relieved from her vows as a member of the order of the Sisters of Loretta.

In her statement to the press, she said:

> I have struggled to understand whether the vow of obedience limits one's ability to commit oneself to responsibilities which are largely outside the domain of the hierarchical church. . . . I have come to believe that the notion of the cloister—in physical enclosure or in social regulations or in dress—is not valid for some of us who must live our lives as dedicated women in the public forum.

Her involvement in the pushing and shoving of life went far beyond the expected agenda for a nun who was president of a Church college. She has been a vital contributor in leadership to the Peace Corps, to urban slum projects, and on the front line of educational experiments with other universities and foundations. The theater that she established with the support of Conrad Hilton on the Webster campus hardly restricted itself to themes from the "Singing Nun" or isolated acts from morality plays of the Middle Ages.

What will her strategy be, how does she define her new position? In one statement she remarked:

> Whenever you expend your energy defending positions—as the Church did for so long—you lose the spirit of free inquiry. Now the whole concept of the Church is changing and it will never be the same—thank the Lord.

Then she touched on the meaning of her witness, both in academic communities and on the sidewalks of St. Louis:

> Convinced of the power of religious presence as distinct from religious control, we wish to demonstrate to an open and opening world, and to ourselves, that the vital force of faith can live and mature in a dynamic society.

Out of all the flurry and, at times, fury of the present religious dishevelment we will see the emergence of new men and women of faith. Not fearful or hesitant or cringing, but faithful ones who have the nerve to believe that this is God's world. That, with Teilard de Chardin, "we go to meet him who comes." That the One who is the God and Father of Abraham, Isaac, and Jacob is also part of the present moment and will be there in the next. And not restricted to the secure surroundings, the predictable Gothic patterns of the past.

One God

And there is no manual for the secular.

Sometimes this is explained to us in the vision of the artist: his translations of reality give expression to our stumbling, awkward definitions. It was what Richard Niebuhr of Yale Divinity School must have meant when he said that the Christian had to learn to improvise in his ethical encounters. The Kingdom of Love does not always yield to lists of mimeographed options.

I believe that artist Charles Schorre touched on this when he described the meaning of religious experience:

> The movies *Patch of Blue* and *Zorba the Greek* were religious experiences for me; I have also had them in churches, in the kitchen washing dishes with my wife, with my children in the backyard, with persons in strange places, with a life class in a university.

Perhaps he should have stopped here, and not tempted those who are the border guards of heresy by saying:

> Are we saved: It is up to each of us to live up to our salvation with all we have in us, to be with all our being. If we don't we are slobs, slopping through life, no matter how clever, beautiful, rich, lucky, talented, charitable, or religious.

Those who pull back in alarm—later to become shock, and then its stepsister, criticism—have announced that those who plunge so cleverly into the world will only receive its stain and not find the Savior. Their argument contends that some social gains are won at the loss of spiritual development and strength of soul. Activity on the surface, they claim, hides a shallow spirit, an undisciplined vulgarity.

I cannot speak for others, but part of my own adventure in the world has confirmed the presence of God as well as His enemies. The movement of the Holy Spirit, according to scripture, is a leading into the spirit of wisdom and might, the spirit of understanding and love, the spirit of the fear of the Lord.

If this truly be God's world, then He shall not be confined to the traditions of our collective experience or the dictates of nineteenth-century piety. He is the One who chooses to reveal Himself to men. If this be true, then the secular saint will not be tormented by the hiddenness of God, but inspired by His presence.

Did the Psalmist anticipate our times in his moment when he cried:

> If I ascend to heaven, thou art there!
> If I make my bed in Sheol, thou art there!
> If I take the wings of the morning and dwell
> in the uttermost parts of the sea,
> even there thy hand shall lead me,
> and thy right hand shall hold me.
>
> If I say, "Let only darkness cover me,
> and the light about me by night,"
> even the darkness is not dark to thee,
> the night is bright as the day;
> for darkness is as the light with thee.

Indeed, the God and Father of Sarah and Abraham is also the One over Cape Kennedy and Waikiki.

The Sins of the Secular Involvement

The variety and intensity of thoughtful people launching into the secular arena have not always been fruitful or inspiring. Some seem to think that divine truth is magnified by taking secular events—almost at whim—polishing them to a religious veneer, and wham—you have a twentieth-century achievement in spiritual discovery. The other half of this kind of thinking belongs to those who believe in the use of obvious, massive symbolism to proclaim the eternal truths of God and the personal claims of Christ. . . . Such as the large neon cross that was erected on an Oregon hillside (recently taken down by court order, judges sometimes being merciful as well as just) and the late adventure in Florida. Here a five-hundred-foot aluminum cross has been erected and it is not yet decided if piety, spirituality, and Christian influence have gained in relationship to the hours that the symbol has stood.

What we may not have recognized is the distorted message that emerges from the overuse of symbolism that had vitality and meaning a half century ago. The power of God is still a throbbing, soaring, dynamic, eternal force in the universe. How pathetic the Christian is who resorts to nostalgic and confusing symbols to express his faith!

Peter De Vries touched on this irony in one of his books. He wrote in the *Mackeral Plaza* about the weird neon sign that had been planted so confidently in a city square, flashing its tireless (and tiring) message:

Jesus Saves—Jesus Saves—Jesus Saves

One wonders if it is related to a bank or savings and loan society.

A New York subway poster caught this mood when someone scribbled "Jesus Saves but Moses Invests." An irreverence that suggests the irrelevance of outworn or unused vocabulary of faith.

Alas, the surge to be relevant and swinging in a secular culture has not shown such a thrilling improvement to date.

The temptation is to be clever, quoted, and "in" with the beautiful people, whoever they are. The sin of stuffiness leads to an overreaction against the obvious mistakes of King James piety that have smothered so many others. But how far do we go in new adventures in relevance and religion? Pretty far if some are to be the new standard-bearers.

The Dangers of Irreverent Prayer

One direction that has been acclaimed is the notion that a certain amount of irreverence might as well be practiced by Christians, since everybody else is scoring well with it. This night-club-supper-club humor has brought guffaws from the jet set, so why not from the pew, goes the argument.

Why not? For my money, the losses exceed the gains. The illustration of this seems invariably to pop out in different attempts to write a banquet invocation or a luncheon-club litany. Occasionally, they are just great. Often they are a disaster. Such as:

> Almighty God, our Father and Friend—we are well aware that we have a lot in common. You want the same market we want in order to stay in business. You want the same things we want—consumer acceptance, honest feedback and good ratings. Well, since we are in the same type of business perhaps we should get to

know each other a little better—there isn't a professional theologian in the crowd, but with Your talent and our know-how, we could corner the market.

Some people say You're dead—don't feel too bad—almost everybody in this room, worth their salt, has been declared dead at one time or another. It's part of the game when your target is the fickle market known as man. Besides, You're not dead, it's just Your image that's being refocused. Your contract hasn't been canceled, it's just being negotiated. We've heard this line before, God, and it's nice to know we have so much in common. So now that we've established contact, discovered our relationship, joined the same fraternity, let's become partners. We really need each other!

Here's the pitch—

Help me be a real "pro" and I'll give you prime time. I know that in your eyes, a real "pro" is dedicated, seeks perfection, honors others' ideas, tries to be honest, seeks success but admits failure, and above all doesn't live because others die!

Well, now that our script is plainly written for all to see,

Let's enjoy our meal and pray for the FCC.

Amen.

Others speak of secular involvement when they have used the vocabulary of the shopping plaza and clubhouse to convey some divine truth. Slang is considered a smooth agent of the spirit. Slogans take the place of scripture. The attempt to be clever does not hide the shallowness of theology or the failure of reaching a depth where the explosions really count.

We have suffered a rash of "prayers" in public life.

Not the awful ones that open political conventions, dedicate livestock shows, or precede the Sugar Bowl classic, but one like this that was given large play in the popular press last year:

> O God, the author and exemplar of poise, power, perseverance and pointedness, give us a portion of your smoothness and accuracy on the golf course.
>
> Make all our shots long and true, all our putts square and plunky, and all our thoughts and words decent and charitable.
>
> Make us meek and humble, amiable, and unselfish, careful, kind and conversational with the golf course. And may we carry all these God-like qualities with us wherever we go.
>
> Bless all who play this course. Bless our champions, our duffers, our par-ers, our birdies, and our quadruple bogies. May they all golf in a spirit of fun, charity, humility and respect for your name. May golf make them better men and bring them closer to you . . . and one day, Lord, bring them all to your green pastures where all shots will be straight and true and all scores will be pars, birds and eagles.

(Yes, I believe in prayer. I believe in praying for people, for football players, for pregnant women, for those dying in rest homes. But this praying before a game . . . you say, we pray not for victory, but that we will do our best. That the best team will win, that no one will degrade himself or another through foul or fraud. Good. But how come the teams always pray just before the game but never in practice . . . ?)

Bishop Fulton J. Sheen once told the New York State Legislature:

> I'm not going to pray for you. There are certain things a man does for himself. He has to blow his own nose, make his own love and say his own prayers.

The Gospel According to Peanuts

The obvious difficulties arise when we try to read too much into popular figures that dominate the public mind. They change quickly from year to year, almost according to Nielsen Ratings, Academy Award nominations, or the Top Ten from Variety.

By too much, I mean that although there are significant themes of Christian ideals in the comic strips like Peanuts, it is easy to overpreach on every episode.

In the *Gospel According to Peanuts,* the author states that the appearance of rain means God's love (His rain falls on the just and the unjust), and the Tree (which shelters, protects, makes houses, a Cross) is something to lean on in trouble.

The swinging little beagle, Snoopy, is a Christian aid. If the central Christian virtues are loving, caring, patience, steadfastness, courage, then Snoopy wins by two long floppy ears.

Yet Robert Short goes on to promote the image of this kennel clown into a Christ figure because he loves people, punctures pride, and lifts up the broken-hearted. Enlarging on this and probably looking for some biblical support for the thesis he has kited, Short comments:

> . . . the dog also is a good symbol of faith as there is a real sense in which a man must become "as a dog" before he can become a Christian. Hegel said that of all creatures, then, the most religious must be the dog.

Here we see an attempt to bridge the gap between a secular illustration and a biblical truth. Dogs simply were not, in spite of Short's statement, highly regarded in the scriptures. Aside from a few chosen sheepdogs, the place of the dog in scripture is despised. And not as a Christ figure, forsaken or rejected, but because dogs were usually wild packs of vicious animals that would attack livestock, children, and the dying.

When the term is used in I Samuel 17:43, the reference is one of contempt. In other Old and New Testament references too many to number, a dog means the enemy, a worthless object, the wicked, and plotters of evil. And in Deuteronomy it means a male temple prostitute. There was no canine registry in Jerusalem and when a person went to the dogs, it was not the Westminster Show in Madison Square Garden, but the final approach to death.

In fact, one of the embellishments in the story of Lazarus was not meant to be an endorsement for a litter of Snoopys—rather, a condemnation of how low they had allowed their brother to fall in his illness ("Lazarus, full of sores . . . moreover the dogs came over and licked his sores").

In his book *Tomorrow's Church,* William A. Holmes describes a special youth service to commemorate the thirteen-year-old age group in the church. While I generally laud the adventurous and at times courageous activities of this Dallas, Texas, congregation, the litany from Peanuts by Mrs. Ruth Turner is but another example of kneeling at the shrine of comic-strip art.

Prayer of Confession (prayed by the young people following the cartoon discussion):

Almighty God, Father of our Lord Jesus Christ, maker of all things, judge of all men: We acknowledge and bewail our manifold sins and wickedness.
Like Lucy—
We look for a scapegoat.
We demand that the world be perfect.
We are determined to "walk over people before they walk over us."
We want life to be "yes, yes, yes" with no "downs."
Like Charlie Brown—
We've been confused from the day we were born.
We feel out of place on the earth.
We feel unloved.
The Goat in us rises instead of the hero.
We're wishy-washy.
Like Snoopy—
We make great plans and put them off until after supper.
We try to be something we aren't, as he pretends to be a wolf, a vulture, or a penguin.
Like Linus—
No problem is so big or so complicated that it can't be run away from.

We expect nothing as a gift, but feel it has
to be earned.
We need a blanket.
We can't face life unarmed.
We sit in the pumpkin patch waiting for the
wrong savior.
The whole trouble with us is—we won't listen
to what the whole trouble with us is.

This scanning of the secular entertainment field for Christian verification is not the fuzziness of any one denomination. Writing in the August 1966 issue of *St. Anthony Messenger,* a regular columnist known as Big Sister decided to give Batman and Robin the Peanuts theological massage.

The Dynamic Duo

Batman is this year's TV craze. Soon a new series of adventures in Gotham City will be starting. This summer we have had to be content with watching re-runs. Last week's episodes featured the Cat Woman. This "cunning culprit" stole some priceless jeweled cats and led the "dynamic duo" (Batman and Robin, of course) on a merry chase.

The closing scene found Cat Woman clinging to the ledge of a bottomless pit with one hand. In the other hand she clutched the priceless cats. The "caped crusader" (Batman) offered to throw a life-saving rope to the "frantic feline." However, she would have had to drop the treasured cats to catch the rope. As you bat fans know, she refused to surrender the wealth, lost her grip on the ledge and plunged to her death. Exit Cat Woman!

This bat caper reminded Big Sister of the Gospel according to St. Mark, chapter 6, verse 24: At that time, Jesus said to his disciples: "No man can serve two masters; for either he will hate the one and love the other, or else he will stand by the one and despise the other. You cannot serve God and mammon."

Batman offered the live-saving rope to Cat Woman. Christ offers us the lifeline of grace. However, we have to drop our "priceless cats"—our sinful habits—if we want to catch this rope. Sometimes we think we can have both. We forget what Christ has said: "No man can serve two masters."

Most of us have a firm grip on the ledge. We are in the state of sanctifying grace. The less Christlike we are, the weaker our grip becomes and the heavier becomes the weight that is dragging us into the bottomless pit—hell.

Cat Woman had her salvation within her fingers' reach. She just had to drop the treasure to catch the rope. Instead, she was greedy and lost her life. She had nothing in the end. If we do not have Christ's life in us when we die, we will have nothing for eternity but the pain of hell. "What does it profit a man if he gains the whole world, yet suffers the loss of his soul?"

We are working for a happy ending to our episode of life on earth. If we team up with Christ, we cannot help but be a "dynamic duo."

In the Batman episodes of comic-book fame, there are plenty of readers who question the normalcy of the relationship between Batman and Robin, as well as their representation of a doubtful masculinity. Suddenly to plunge young—and old—readers into total endorsement of a Batman and Robin partnership—as being comparable to Jesus Christ and the believer—is mocking both religion and secular comics.

Albert Outler may have the summary that says it all:

> Surely, somewhere in the pondering of our fears and hopes it might occur to a really open mind that the current consensus amongst the self-styled "moderns" is really too facile, that the capacity of the Christian tradition to renew its relevance in a world come of age has been underrated, that Christianity's talk of providence is more than a cosmic analogy of Linus's blanket.

«2»

Remodel or Rebuild or Remove?

I have always felt that those who were caustic and critical about the church, sharp in their comments, and able to reach vehemence in their statements really had a lover's quarrel with the cathedral. If they really didn't give a damn, they wouldn't be looking in its direction: they simply would pass by and cause the whole enterprise to be invisible to their inmost feelings.

But there are many who are so angry with the church because they love it so deeply. Not the ivy and the organ. Not the little church games of etiquette and propriety. Rather, the awesome, stirring challenge to set the lives of men in the exalting scenery of the beauty and truth of life. To display the fierce honesty and the flashing word that give life its dimension. To kindle again those bright flames of hope for the world now and the world to come, for they both belong to God. It's underachievement that is killing the church. Tiny faith, dwarfed hope, and diluted love are all there and this is a sickening diet of what the church might be—and should be!

Frequently the word we say about religion is going to be a word against religion. Tillich said it that way. So did Bernard Shaw, when he wrote to the Sisters of Stanbrook Abbey in England. He had hurt some of his close friends within the church by his tactics. He sought to clarify his strategy by saying:

> In the outside world from which you have escaped it is necessary to shock people violently to make them think seriously about religion; and my ways were too rough. But that was how I was inspired.

Shaw of course was heartened by the appearance of so noble and so rugged a figure as Dean William Ralph Inge.

"It is now clear," said Shaw, "that the Church can be saved, if it is not past salvation, only by men of character and mental force enough to be able to say such things without conscious audacity. Whether the Dean will stay in it when he has saved it is not quite a foregone conclusion. His treasure is in a wider region than the Church of England, or any other such local makeshift;

and where his treasure is, there must his heart be also."

But Shaw gave another side of the inner spirit that drove him on—not to topple the church bell or undermine its tower. But to claim the highest aspiration that the visible mortar and brick and bell church could offer:

> Any place where men dwell, village or city, is the reflection of the consciousness of every single man. In my consciousness there is a market, a garden, a dwelling, a workshop, a lover's work—above all, a cathedral. My appeal to the master builder is: Mirror this cathedral for me in enduring stone; make it with hands; let it direct its sure and clear appeal to my senses, so that when my spirit is vaguely groping after an elusive mood my eye shall be caught by the skyward tower, showing me where, within the cathedral, I may find my way to the cathedral within me.

Antoine de Saint-Exupéry, in his *Wind, Sand and Stars,* offers a text that need not embarrass us:

> To be a man is to feel that through one's own contribution one helps build the world.

Many felt this to be the central theme of the Expo '67. I felt this, in another setting, when I was startled by the emotions that welled up as we passed through the Vatican pavilion at the 1964 World's Fair in New York. Here was that wide-angle room filled with quotations, scripture verses, and important ideas. And the best by Martin Buber—"All real living is meeting."

So—it is the encounter, the contribution, the individual

effort to participate in creation that is the essence of what laymen can be about.

Signs of Opposition

All about us are the ugly signs of the opposition. The polluted stream, the foul air, the pornographic paperback, and the latest casualty reports. In his powerful volume *The Myth and the Machine,* Lewis Mumford finds that awful parallel between Egypt and Vietnam, the Nile and Mekong deltas. Under the Sixth Dynasty of Pharaoh Pepi I he records:

> "The army returned in safety
> After it had hacked up the land of the
> Sand Dwellers
> . . . After it had thrown down its enclosures . . .
> After it had cut down its fig trees and vines . . .
> After it had cast fire into all dwellings . . .
> After it had killed troops in it by many
> ten-thousand."

Several years ago Ignazio Silone wrote a piercing essay on world conditions. His concern was not for the obvious questions which worry everyone: the Bomb, Birth Control, or Air Pollution. Nor was he wrestling with the scars of the Cold War, the seductions of Pop Art, or the devaluation of the British pound. Hardly. He was in real anguish over the number of suicides that happened in the careers of so many writers. In almost every instance these men of letters had confided to their friends that they were caught in despair with the futility of life.

Said Silone:

> The last forty years have witnessed the collapse of most of the great politico-social myths bequeathed to us by the 19th century. As a result, certain kinds of people who had relied on these myths as a compass find themselves in a state of spiritual vagueness and ambiguity that is still far from being clarified.

Silone says this crisis is a continuing struggle between capitalism and communism—but there was something even more involved than this conflict of ideology. At heart, he sensed a spiritual malaise, the victory of nihilism, and the frightening advance of Nietzsche's philosophy.

Silone traces the disaster of World War I—and it was a disaster, for the victors enjoyed no world of peace and the victims became the proving ground for dictators and tyrannies like the world had never seen.

"The war," said Silone, "merely demonstrated how fragile were the myths of progress on which capitalist civilization was based. Even in the victorious countries venerable institutions were subjected to such terrible ordeals that they began to totter like rotten scaffolding. And from them, skepticism and corruption spread and seeped downwards to the very foundation of society. Traditional moral and religious values, rashly invoked to prop up the vested interests which were being threatened, were thereby compromised."

It was almost twenty years after World War II that the skepticisms prophesied by Ignazio Silone hit the theological scene in North America. Then it came in 1966 with a rush in the writings and appearances of the Death of God theologians. William Hamilton, Thomas J. Altizer, and interpreters like Paul Van Buren and Gabriel Vahanian seemed to own the book publishers as well as the TV program directors with their message for modern man.

The God is Dead Rocket

Like a massive Cape Kennedy lift off, the God is Dead rocket flashed into the heavens, dazzling the bewildered believer, entertaining the agnostic, and infuriating seminary colleagues. After all, said many scholars, Nietzsche had been around for a century, why should these bright, nervy professors make such a big thing out of it? But they did. Paperbacks flooded the market. *Time* magazine honored the theme with an Easter cover. Hamilton hosted a brief television series. Altizer nearly grounded the fund raising efforts of Emory University as it cajoled alumni to pledge now and believe later.

One sentence does it:

> There was once a God to whom adoration, praise and trust were appropriate, possible, even necessary, but now there is no such God. . . .

This was the essential theme of the God is Dead school. It wavered between the nihilism of Nietzsche, the torments of Dostoyevsky, and the mournful cries of Albert Camus.

These men were all within a younger age bracket. Too old to be cynics, too young to be saints, they crashed into the theological centers with rash statements like Paul Tillich not going far enough and falling back on Bonhoeffer when they had disposed of Barth. Sooner or later the institutional question would be asked, so William Hamilton answered it for everyone listening:

> It must be clear that this theology has neither the power nor the ability to serve the Protestant Church in its present institutional forms. I do not see how preaching, ordination, the sacraments can be taken seriously by radical theologians.

Unfortunately, many felt that the radical theologians were not taking life seriously. The whole discussion seemed to be a parlor discussion gone haywire. To the dismay of the DOG theologians, there was no following or "school." A few fiery debates were held on different campuses, distressed adult church school classes wrung their hands over the discussion theme, and the agony of the contemporary world rolled on. For a year and a half it obliterated the church's consideration of the Vietnam conflict, the shape-up of Black Power, and the pursuit of the ecumenical vision.

As I wrote during that debate:

> In a time when LSD is being used in 16 New York City high schools, when the KKK announces spring rallies for New Jersey and the Watts area of Los Angeles is ready to give us another TV spectacular, in color, the appalling distractions of the God is Dead theologians become even more frightening.

Yet the murmurings, the warnings, the confessions of Ignazio Silone haunt us. "Mankind," he said, "today is in poor shape. Any portrait of modern man, if at all faithful to the original, cannot but be deformed, split, fragmentary, in a word, tragic."

Erich Fromm was on the same wave length when he looked at the tragic scene so described:

> A man sits in front of a bad television program and does not know he is bored; he reads of Vietcong casualties in the newspaper and does not recall the teachings of religion; he learns the dangers of nuclear holocaust and does not feel fear; he joins the rat race of commerce where a person's worth is measured in terms of market values and is not aware of anxiety. Ulcers speak louder than the mind.
>
> Theologians and philosophers have been saying for a century that God is dead, but what we confront now is the possibility that man is dead, transformed into a thing, a producer, a consumer, an idolator of other things.

So these are the times, the framework of the church's existence, the skyline of its heavens: shaped by the TV antenna, the mushroom cloud of Hiroshima, and the friendly skies of United.

The Collapse of Theological Liberalism

You must understand the collapse of theological liberalism in the advent and events of World War II. Liberalism, with its allies of science and most branches of higher education, was able to overpower the dominant fundamentalist church forces and thinkers around War I.

For the quarter century following, theological liberalism led by Harry Emerson Fosdick, Norman Thomas, the Niebuhrs (at first), and latter-day followers of Walter Rauschenbusch was able to control the destiny of American Protestant thought. Society was improvable. Western society was the source of decent social and political reform; citizens of North America as well as Europe were ready to bask in the fruits of a Christendom that had built cathedrals, blessed empires, and battled the heathen.

The house wrecking began in the unpleasant disintegration of the European overseas empires which fell in during the World War II conflict.

The greatest shock of all was the rise of Adolf Hitler —spawned not in the wretched slums of Bagdad nor weaned in the ghettos of China or Mongolia, but a gleaming uniformed product of an outwardly Christian culture that had the academic awards, scientific honors, musical prowess, medical ingenuity, and social graces of the highest rank.

The cultural heritage that had produced an Einstein, Barth, Brunner, Beethoven, Bach, Bonhoeffer, the Niebuhrs—had become also the epitome of evil and wickedness.

It is a fact that six million Jews were gassed, stacked, and burned by a Christian culture. This decade of defilement marked the end of Christendom—not the gospel, not the Christian way, not the loving fellowship or forgiving spirit, but the Christendom which had been the trustful caretaker for man since the persuasive Constantine, through ages dark and bright, empire building and universal church in command.

In reality, Karl Barth, Richard and Reinhold Niebuhr, and especially Dietrich Bonhoeffer sawed the legs off the scaffolding of Christendom. That majestic structure, which had been fashioned almost by whim under Constantine, which tottered through the Dark Ages, was beguiled by the Renaissance, convulsed in the Reformation, rejuvenated by empire expansion, is now at bay everywhere.

For God is in the revolution, the alienation, the overthrow, the protest, the little people in the square who are shaking their umbrellas at the establishment everywhere.

Bonhoeffer saw this through the window of his cell. Here he has been buried for nearly a quarter of a century and students carry his paperback writings in their Levis and Honda saddlebags.

So young Bonhoeffer spoke, as the German church cracked, splintered, and dissolved before Hitler's mauling thrust.

It was in 1932 that Bonhoeffer perceived enough of the Nazi movement and its death embrace with the Christian community to say:

> No man builds the Church but Christ alone. Whoever is minded to build the church is surely well on the way to destroying it, for he will build a temple to idols without wishing or knowing it. . . . We must proclaim—He builds. We must pray to him that he may build. We do not know his plan. We cannot see whether he is

building or pulling down. It may be that the times which by human standards are times of collapse are, for him, the great times of construction.

Perhaps our world and our church and our vision became very different when we began to absorb the shock and shame that Western society had achieved in the Hitler period: as diverse as an Anne Frank and Adolph Eichmann (who, like his mentor Adolf Hitler, never smoke or drank).

Is this what Nelly Sachs meant when she wrote her poem, "O the Chimneys":

O the chimneys
O the ingeniously devised habitations of death
When Israel's body drifted as smoke
Through the air—
Was welcomed by a star, a chimney sweep,
A star burned black
Or was it a ray of sun?

O the chimneys!
Freedomway for Jeremiah and Job's dust—
Who devised you and laid stone upon stone
The road for refugees of smoke?

O the habitations of death,
Invitingly appointed
For the host who sued to be a guest—
O you fingers
Laying the threshold
Like a knife between life and death—

O you chimneys,
O you fingers
And Israel's body as smoke through the air!

The Noise of Small Sounds

People are now today concerned about so many things. What does the collapse of Sunday School mean more than anything else—that adults are unable to understand or ask the moral question?

As Roger Hazelton wrote in *A Theological Approach To Art,* "The mystery which dwells in the heart of the Christian faith is too vast, too inexhaustible, too auspicious for the human journey, to be hobbled and crippled any longer in dead forms."

As indicators, the individual is going to be prepared, if his vision of God is real and his sensitivity growing, going to go against the stream—against the prevailing mood, uphill against the religious etiquette, the corporation code of ethics, the patriotic recipes—and be his own man if he is to be God's man. The Group is becoming a death threat—the uniform, a spiritual imprisonment. All uniforms.

Again Nelly Sachs, Nobel Prize winner, asks the religious question for the devout as well as the non-believer when she inquires:

> If the prophets broke in
> through the doors of night
> and sought an ear like a homeland—
>
> Ear of mankind
> overgrown with nettles,
> would you hear?
> If the voice of the prophets
> blew

on flutes made of murdered children's bones
and exhaled airs burnt with
martyrs' cries—
if they built a bridge of old men's dying
groans—

Ear of mankind
occupied with small sounds,
would you hear?

The small sounds have us by the ears.

Why has this become such a prime era of ecclesiastical dishevelment, theological ferment, and religious hell raising?

What kind of time is this when a Marxist Passolini does an award-winning film on the life of Christ in "The Gospel According to St. Matthew"?

What kind of political-religious irony is it that the amendment proposed by the Roman Catholic Church to the New York State Constitution granting aid and assistance to the parochial schools will be defeated because half of the Catholics will vote against it?

How do you describe the life and fellowship of the church when on a Sunday evening Malcolm Boyd addresses a standing-room audience of 1,200 souls in New York and opens his sermon by saying that he wants first to talk about the goddam war in Vietnam.

Indeed, the theological, ecclesiastical revolution is on when personalities like Bishop Pike outdraw Melvin Belli and Mark Lane in student gatherings at Ann Arbor, Michigan.

A Churchly Silence

But the deeper question is surely an amazement at the institutional church for such emotional disarray, with the Vatican urging priests to stop arguing celibacy, to cool it in regard to folk masses, to beg married couples to give the church more time concerning the birth control question, and the underground church to turn in its arms and equipment in a sort of religious amnesty.

I do not mean for a moment to wrap the Roman Church with all the flypaper of change, rather to give an overview of what I think is happening in all branches of the organized church—hoping to discern the cause and source of this massive uneasiness, discontent, and spreading secularism.

Michael Novak, brilliant spokesman for the new shape of the coming Christian community, has succinctly etched the outline of the historic problem:

> Christianity was for a period the religion of Western culture; by the time the civilization of that period decayed and its deficiencies became apparent, Christianity was so identified with the past that it seemed unable to survive the breakthrough of the West toward a new form of civilization. Bishops who live in princely palaces; religious metaphors borrowed from an agricultural society; a church authority whose conceptions of obedience and freedom are feudal or baroque; an ethic shaped by and shaping the interests of the middle classes—these remain today as the residue of the past.

There can be little doubt where this double standard is leading: one mode will survive the other, and I vote for the contemporary statement. Some contend that modern man should be able to straddle the problem of the historic, nostalgic formula while fastening down the new implications of a more lively expression. Daniel Callahan has proposed for consideration that twentieth-century Christians maintain their historic ties to the one great church while getting their social action and/or esoteric expression through some sect or group. Thus the mainline thrust of Christianity is preserved and the front line allowed to swing with its own improvisations and techniques that elude the majority.

So, indeed, the ferment within the church is also a result of the failure of the church.

Another important factor has been the breakdown of absolute authority, absolute truth, absolute sureness in the mood of the ecumenical movement. With this happening, there had been a fantastic thing about not wanting to proselytize, etc.

On the contrary, a writer like Martin Buber has brought so much wisdom and insight to all men that Christians find their uniqueness dissolved in his company and blessed by his thought. Said Buber:

> God is to be seen in everything and reached by every pure deed.

In the searing play, *The Deputy*, we have the implication of Pope Pius XII in the death of the European Jews under Hitler.

Rolf Hochhuth, the author of the play, in responding to a student forum at Columbia, said:

> I challenge the position of the Pope because he was the person who had the highest moral obligation. He was also that person who even in material and social matters had the greatest influence.

Against all questions and challenges raised by the students, said Albert H. Friedlander in *Never Trust a God Over 30*, Hochhuth maintained that the Pope as God's deputy had to speak out against the evil of Hitler's concentration camps. Three years of research had convinced the author that the Pope's silence condemned Jews to death, that the voice of the Vatican would have slowed the work of extermination to some extent, and that Pius XII had to be called to account for his silence.

One of the things you discover about the church is the fact that most members and ministers are not going to speak out on a social issue. . . . In the case of the clergy, let us take a professional who has spent a good part of his life trying to help people get on. His efforts and energies at marital reconciliations, parent-youngster quarrels, interboard squabbles, and congregational splits have left him rather winded and leery when it comes to the application of a piercing insight on some social question.

How much tension does he want to have beyond the daily round?

The other factor is a practical one. How much time does one have to prepare on the Vietnam war, the struggle of Black Power, the scientific and military elite, the New Morality, and the old cemetery mores? Not a lot. And the pastor is not going to make a fool of himself as he weaves in and out of the social gospel maze. Silence is not proud but at least it is more prudent than a half-baked pronouncement, goes the feeling.

Churches and Social Issues

The Presbytery of Hudson River asked its 112 churches to consider several questions about the Vietnam war. When the Presbytery committee charged with reporting the results tallied its returns, they were sad, to say the least. Only eight churches bothered to respond. Two said that the church should stick to the gospel and forget politics. Two others gave an indistinct sigh. Six churches favored a statement of some direction and leadership from the Presbytery and that was it.

When the Presbytery of Tulsa spoke out concerning the discriminatory practices of Oklahoma society, especially in regard to public accommodations for Negroes, only one church did anything specific about it. John Knox Presbyterian Church picketed several of the leading restaurants and asked its members to refrain from supporting the establishments. Their letter read:

> Dear Sirs:
>
> As members of John Knox Presbyterian Church, believing that any practice that interferes with the right of any person to full opportunity to be regarded as a child of God is contrary to the Christian conscience, the undersigned come pleading that you reconsider your

business policy of refusing service to human beings on the basis of the God-given color of their skin.

We are mindful of the accomplishments all of Tulsa has made in the direction without a law, but we are also aware that your resistance to the principles of the Public Accommodations Resolution are a major roadblock to a peaceful and equitable resolution of this concern.

We acknowledge your rights as a property owner of a successful business that has grown with Tulsa, but we believe that your policy of discrimination involves an area that transcends property rights and man-made laws. Because of our convictions, we will not be able to patronize your establishment until this policy has been revised. As ones who are seeking to be responsible and obedient disciples of Jesus Christ, we respectfully request your reconsideration.

It was touching and trying. They were alone.

The pastor and the parish are up tight on so many concerns that only the tiniest minority is going to exert moral leadership and say the social word to a gasping and groping society. Perhaps that is all right.

One of my theories is that leaders of national or regional influence are allowed one or two areas of authority and respect. They might extend their interest to other fields, in rare exceptions be a "Renaissance man" and capture several or more. But usually you are allowed one or two major lines and that's it. Let me explain.

When Wilt Chamberlain admitted that he was considering the world of professional boxing, nobody wrote for tickets. Why? He is Mr. Basketball. His court play, team effort, and personal excellence are unsurpassed. Honor and fame and cash have flooded in. But boxing? He was about as welcome as a giraffe at a dog show. He had found and claimed his place in the sports world and in the heart of the fans on the basketball court. He got the message.

Do you recall the news item that appeared before the national political conventions of 1964 stating that, in spite of the rumors, Billy Graham would not consider an invitation to be on a party ticket? It was almost funny. The public has long shown its interest and support of Graham as evangelist and preacher in countless religious meetings and services. But there was never any public discussion of his possible candidacy.

The result would be embarrassing to the public and disastrous to the evangelist. For just that reason Pope Paul would never stand for election to the Italian Parliament. One field, yes—two, no.

The Role of the Local Minister

This is true on delicate social issues and the role of a local minister. A congregation or community will respond to their pastor if he takes a strong stand, say, on fair housing. It won't be pleasant and the strain soon separates the bigots from the believers. But, generally, the congregation will take it *if* he doesn't suddenly turn up the volume on the church's paying taxes or getting rid of the choir director or calling for the burning of draft cards. These other issues may be just as important to him but he wisely learns to pace himself, like the dentist who drills and then cools.

This is what is happening to Bishop Pike. His interest, concern, involvement in so many social-religious-ethical debates have brought him to the credibility gap with his friends and the public.

Being a person of such unusual charm and such a towering intellect, Pike seems to have been given by the public at least three or four issues to employ. So he has had some pretty thrilling times as the front runner on things like reform of abortion laws, the New Morality, birth control, the experimental use of drugs, and better understanding for homosexuals. When time permitted, he also reworked the creeds of his church, discussed the death of God, and outlined new moves for peace in Vietnam. But then my Wilt Chamberlain theory came into practice. To be a professional in one area does not mean expertise in another—say spiritualism.

Every family in the pew and plenty out in the parish have had strong feelings in this field and they didn't need a bishop to straighten them out. Historically, spiritualism is so riddled with fraud, deceit, and foolishness that Pike added nothing new to their knowledge except a suspicion about where he is heading. What next, they are asking.

The true Renaissance man was gifted in art, music, and theater, and enjoyed one more quality—he knew when to stop and reflect on his work.

When you look at the American prophetic vision, there have been only a handful—fistful—of those who stood above the pack and the party to say the clear, cutting word that divides the right and the wrong. That is how things are now—religiously. There is presently not one national ecclesiastical figure who will go against the grain. Into the wind. Upstream. Since things are so bleak, it may mean that a new breed is about to come forward in leadership. But these are the last years of the church as we know it.

The Impact of the Institutional Church

We would do well to study the impact of the institutional church on the world about it. Michael Novak sorted out some of the clerical dilemmas when he observed:

> The clean-shaven monsignori who run the chancery, the school system, the seminaries, and the largest parishes, seem to be businessmen, golfers, connoisseurs of restaurants, well trained to the books of canon law, in love with the Church as an institution, money raisers, enemies of secularism, proud of the church as a bulwark against atheistic communism, good company for brother priests and for congenial parishioners, sometimes prayerful, and faithful eunuchs of the kingdom of God . . . the younger clergy are full of promise, whereas large numbers of the laity appear to have long ago been poisoned by the invisible, odorless gas of apathy. The problem no longer is lay versus clerical. The problem now is life of the spirit versus death. Many priests, as well as laymen, are suffering in the night of faith; they find it difficult to believe that God is alive in the people who continue to fill the churches. Many priests and sisters are empty of consolation.

It's hard not to have short breath and a quick pulse when you realize how far we have ranged from many of the central themes of the New Testament. It's difficult to believe that there ever was a primitive church, a New Testament fellowship, a fresh, clear-eyed gathering of young saints who followed as disciples with nerve and conviction. William Stringfellow, whom many of us consider America's most articulate layman, urges a return to biblical studies as the heart and guidebook for church and believer—the only way for salvation and sanity.

For instance, John 3:16 is universally acclaimed as the most popular and most frequently memorized passage of the Bible. I have no reason to doubt it. The hang-up for me is the gross misemphasis that can develop over any favorite text. John said:

> God so loved the world that he gave his only begotten Son that whoever believes in him should not perish but have eternal life.

Martin Luther called it the gospel in miniature. In this brief paragraph we have the plan and purpose of God in Christ—saving, reclaiming, renewing the world through His Son and those who claim Him in faith.

But do we really snatch the significance of this text for today and our problems of the church? It must have been more than circumstance that the writer of the fourth Gospel included this material where he did—for you note that the passage follows a rather lengthy discourse between Jesus and Nicodemus.

Nicodemus had been a great follower and believer of

Judaism. He was confronted, as a "churchman," with the claims of Christ. This for the first time in his life brought him face to face with the mystery and majesty of God.

This particular passage from John states that God loves the whole world, and to one steeped in the provincial ways of Jewish nationalism and folkways this was indeed a large and extensive thought.

So underline it: God loved the world.

What Does Love Mean?

We ought to collect all the definitions and interpretations of "love" to find the depth of this concept. In the New Testament we know that love can be sacrificial, it may be undeserved, it is found to be strengthening, outgoing, inseparable. Jesus used the word love, and by contrast consider what was *not* said:

> that God loves the roll of church members
> and especially those graduated from church-related colleges
> that God loves and prefers the practices
> of the saints
> that God loves those who help themselves
> that God loves the English-speaking world best
> and America first
> that God loves the Holy Lands and most
> especially those areas west of the Jordan

So, what an astounding and incomprehensible statement. That God loves the world!

This messy mankind with its kings and rogues, its

scholars and dropouts, its streetwalkers and grandmothers, its gladiators and nurses' aides, its Albert Schweitzers and Joseph Stalins, its Martin Luther Kings and Ku Klux Klans.

When the writer of John said the world, he meant the whole created earth, everyone and all, the least and the greatest, the lovely and the hated. He said that it was this world that God did not pity or ignore or detest or resent. He loved it. And how strange and sad that our attention is not directed to the needs and hopes of the world, but to the tax exemptions, privileges, and sighings of the institutional church, which has come to be served, instead of to serve, to be ministered unto, instead of to minister, to save itself in hopes that it will not die.

I don't believe that we will have any lasting or significant change in the marching orders of the church until we have a better grasp of God's concern for the world and the outward-bound momentum of a people following His concern. God didn't love another world. Nor a more receptive or kindly world. It's the piece of earth with its disease and disasters, its sunsets and race riots, its H-bombs and Broadway plays, its church burnings and rose festivals, its protest marches and red-carpet service.

The clergy and the laity need now to become lovers of the world for the sake of Jesus Christ.

One Christian, so admired and revered in this period, has said:

> Man is challenged to participate in the sufferings of God at the hands of a godless world.
>
> He must therefore plunge himself into the life of a

> godless world, without attempting to gloss over its ungodliness with a veneer of religion or trying to transfigure it. He must live a wordly life and so participate in the sufferings of God. . . . To be a Christian does not mean to be religious in a particular way, to cultivate some form of asceticism—but to be a man. It is not some religious act which makes a Christian what he is, but a participation in the suffering of God in the life of the world.

Two days after he wrote that, Dietrich Bonhoeffer was hung for his participation in the world as a Christian who had become an activist in the plot to destroy Adolf Hitler.

The Message Today

What's the Message?

We get the State of the Union message every now and then from the frozen steps of the Capitol.

We get the baccalaureate message from the worn steps of a thousand ivy-covered campuses at graduation time.

We get the message from the convention, the truce teams, the hospital waiting rooms, and the Bankers Trust. When Sugar Ray Robinson knocked out one opponent he was asked about the punch that did it. "Well," remarked the cool champion, "it was a short jab—it only went six inches, but I think he got the message."

We live and die and retreat and succeed on messages of all kinds and sorts.

What is the Message for Today?

Where poverty is, there can never be law or order. *Sean O'Casey*

We need wealth in order to do love and justice. *William Temple*

The first fact that humanity must realize is that the greatest of our evils and the worst of our crimes is poverty. *Bernard Shaw*

The belly comes before the soul, not in the scale of values, but in point of time. *George Orwell*

What is the Message for Today—is it the message of Marshall McLuhan media? Is it the masochistic message that strangled spirits and stunted men, described by William E. Lecky, in his *History of European Morals*, which nevertheless inspired extensive followings and uncounted converts:

> There is, perhaps, no phase in the moral history of mankind of a deeper or more painful interest than this ascetic movement. . . . A hideous, sordid and emaciated maniac, without knowledge, with patriotism, without moral affection, passing his life in a long routine of useless and atrocious self torture, and quailing before ghastly phantoms of his delirious brain, had become the ideal of the nations which had known the writings of Plato and Cicero and the lives of Socrates and Cato.

When Yvonne Seadin Roscow interviewed some successful young businessmen she gleaned these comments from "The Sweet Sweet Life of a Bachelor Ad Man":

> Don't feel compelled to do anything you don't want to do. Don't be afraid of hurting girls' feelings. Girls are easily bruised and easily replaced.

> If you succumb to the idea of a permanent relationship, poll your married friends first. If they don't dissuade you, go to the suburbs and study the women in the supermarkets for a couple of hours.

During the turmoil and tension of the Father Groppi demonstrations in Milwaukee, Victor Hoffman interviewed the priest and members of his NAACP Youth Council. He concluded that James Groppi was an authentic prophet, preaching and teaching in the historic tradition of a Jeremiah, John the Baptist, Savonarola and Dietrich Bonhoeffer. Groppi's target was the Milwaukee City Government and its tight, closed view toward integrated housing. His audience was the world. Hoffman confessed that his encounter with Pastor Groppi persuaded him to ask these questions of the church:

1. What kind of theology must we construct in 1967 or '68 to shape the world in which we live?
2. Does the priest minister only to his parish or does he minister to the total community?
3. What kind of power may a minister or a religious person employ to give himself an effective voice in the community?
4. Is our mission directed only to the soul of man and not to his body?

Those are really fresh questions for the church to ask of itself every year and within quite different situations. How they are answered depends almost entirely on our idea of God and how He has revealed Himself in the Bible, in the life of the church, and in His unfolding creation.

What is the Message?

Can you be your own man or are you forever on the manipulative string of a favorite newcaster, subtle stylist, or incessant boss.

Just what did Herbert L. Mathews mean when he said in his last column for the New York *Times,* just before he retired at the end of August in 1967:

> There is, at least, a residue of satisfaction in thinking that one did not always go the way of the crowd. A newspaperman walks with the great of many lands, but he must go his own way—right to the end of the road.

What about the Message? Everyone is preaching, everyone is reaching for a decision whether it be Billy Graham or Phil Rizzuto.

Some of it is so subtle and constant that you never have a chance to steam off the veneer and discover the real composition underneath. Is that what Marc Golden of CBS meant when he said

> There's one constant in every successful dramatic TV story form, and that's that the leading character's occupation is somehow connected with death.

How Much Freedom?

So everybody cashes in on the death market. Death is fun, so you form karate clubs and teach coeds the ballet of death. And we chop wood with our palms and maim a million would-be assailants. Death is entertainment, successful as "Bonnie and Clyde," who laughed with a machine gun and spilled blood and ice tea with the same indifference. Death is the fun of dying and lying out at Forest Lawn—a place that makes the going great! And the absurd writers tell us that death is God, hoping to revive some new market for overstocked ideas that didn't make it the first time around. And death may be a city, choked in its own polluted water, air, and outlook.

In *The City Church, Death or Renewal,* Walter Kloetzli does a comprehensive study of eight city churches and their response to the challenges, pressures, and problems of urban life. The preparedness of the members of these churches for urban ministry seemed limited and withdrawn. In the afterward of this study, his co-author, Charles Y. Glock, made this conclusion:

> In a constantly changing society, freedom to break with tradition to alter old ways of doing things and to innovate new ones, is almost a prerequisite to serving communities which have been disrupted by urban redevelopment or in which shifts in racial, religious, and social composition have occurred. . . . How much freedom parishioners and the church-at-large are inclined to permit their ministers in meeting the challenge of social change is thus of more than academic importance. Judging from several recent studies which touch on this issue, the answer for parishioners is "not very much."

Does the mood change with fresh young faces, with a new crop of college-trained members, the ranks swelling with business and professional people who are in touch with the megapolis? One answer is:

> Like some scientists, the young executive has little interest in, and less understanding of, liberal arts. In the academic sense, the young executive does not know what the humanities are. He has no grasp of good literature, and no understanding of aesthetics. He has probably not mentioned Keats since he left high school. He does not care, in the phrase of Charles Grosvenor Osgood, to investigate "the operations of the grand laws and mysterious forces that dominate every age: of will and liberty, of pain and retribution, and justice, of love and sacrifice . . ." He does not apprehend works of the imagination. He has never heard the music of the spheres. He would not recognize it if he did.

«3»

The Rise of the Underground

When I was asked to review the book, *Keep The Faith, Baby,* by Adam Clayton Powell, little did I expect to discover that he had been keeping such close company with Halford Luccock and George Buttrick. When I first glanced through the volume of sermons by Congressman Powell, I remarked to a friend that it looked like good preaching. The material was timely. Short sentences and flashing illustrations made for a strong book of sermons. His themes were on the frontier of Christian thought in a revolutionary age: the struggle of the church in the ghetto, the need for repeal of capital punishment, a close appraisal of the political sickness called McCarthyism, how a northern Negro could vote for a white Southerner for President (Johnson).

From beginning to end it was vital, stirring preaching. The kind that warms hearts and fills churches. Unfortunately, I also discovered that several chapters were direct lifts from Halford Luccock of Yale Divinity School and George Buttrick, the pulpit champion, and possibly others.

It was rather surprising to experience the reaction that developed. A high official of the Associated Press asked me if it wasn't common practice for ministers to use other men's published sermons as their own—with or without credit. Others commented that there was no such thing as original material (there are only 120 original ideas in the world, anyway) and that we all were indebted to others for the thoughts and ideas we expressed.

An executive from a church organization said that I had inadvertently assisted in "the lynching of Adam Clayton Powell. He has become the scapegoat of American culture—from Congress to the Press and every small town newspaper editor will gleefully print your exposé." Anyway, reasoned one critic, only two sermons out of forty were lifted or plagiarized, so why spoil a good book.

Perhaps Luccock was right. You shouldn't read the sermons of others because they are too great a temptation. We check their titles, notice the text, and then see the development of illustrations and specific points. It's too easy to dip into another man's work after ten minutes reading—much easier than ten hours of study, reading, and research with original sources.

The Decline of Preaching

But the Powell-*Keep the Faith, Baby* event brought back a deeper concern that I have had for the Christian church in our time: the decline in preaching. Powell quoted or used Luccock and Buttrick. He might have included Fosdick, James Stewart, Leslie Weatherhead, Henry Sloane Coffin. These pulpit greats set the standards for the Christian community for nearly half a century. Yet with their passing we are aware of a steady decline in the power and persuasion of preaching.

The pulpiteer is around but he no longer rules. The big doctors (DD) can be located in our larger cities but they do not dominate the civic landscape or the ecclesiastical power centers. What has allowed this to come to pass in the Christian church, on the American scene especially? Why, all of a sudden, have the greats become names linked with nostalgic spiritual advance?

First, let us understand that we are members of an organizational church. Secondly, we are in service, too often, to support an institutional body. Thirdly, the pastor-preacher has had to become a co-ordinator with this institution-organization. Buildings, annual budgets, twelve choirs, not including bell ringers, scouts, youth groups, women's circles, relocation problems, church parking lots (an entire book has recently been published on this alone—how to control, light, mark, surface, and supervise).

Fosdick said that he spent a minute in the pulpit for every hour of preparation. Or was it the other way around? Either way, the contemporary pastor is more likely to tell you about his case load of counseling, his meeting with the building committee, or the strategy session with the Saul Alinsky Group than the number of hours in the study. This week or last month. His life has changed, and with it, certain opportunities in communication.

The increasing size of most churches today puts a personal load on the back of the pastor. Indeed, he may have a rather large staff to handle his 1,000–2,000-member church. All this means more baptisms, funerals, weddings, calls (telephone, not personal) to nibble at his time and always to be subtracted from his period of Sunday preparation.

The pastor also faces constant and massive competition from every kind of media. People are no longer willing to sit still for a 35–40-minute sermon—even if our man on Sunday had time to prepare it. The listener who has become conditioned to a five-minute newscast and a fifteen-minute quarter in football is not going to support oratory that goes much beyond noon.

Now, if preaching is in decline, so is its first cousin, public speaking. Our body politic is already starting to shudder as it recalls the nominating conventions and the ordeal of political hot air which was called public speaking. It is terrible. Every other sentence is a predictable cliché. If it weren't for the public-address system, the politicians would be drowned out by the conversations and chatter of an indifferent audience.

It may well be that the transistorized PA system, the high-powered microphone, the Teleprompter built into a mechanical lectern are the enemies of good speaking and preaching. Too many people in public life cannot project beyond the first yard of the platform and become literally speechless when threatened with power failure.

What is called for is a return to voice training, a resolve to devote the time required for writing your own material, and a deep yearning to persuade others of the rightness of your cause. If this happens, both church and state will enjoy the benefits.

The All-Powerful Bankbook

In fact, the pastor is expected to deliver most heartily in the field of finances. Does that sound crass, callous, and un-Christian? Perhaps it is, but it also is the oil that turns the machinery. And lubricates.

Most national ecclesiastical boards are filled with men who have proven themselves, but not in New Testament studies, theological research, or pulpit prowess. They are there because they have shown organizational brilliance, institutional loyalty, and fund raising skill. That is the length and depth of too many churches. It is a false standard but it is one that builds.

This is not a special sin of Protestantism. Long ago our Catholic brethren, from bishop to parish priest, learned where the action is. Not the prayer book. The Bankbook. This is what it takes to build cathedrals, extend missions, support Rome, establish parochial schools, enlarge hospitals, remodel seminaries, hold Vatican Councils. Yet this is not accomplished today through preaching or pulpit power. Wasn't it Daniel Moynihan who wrote in *Com-*

monweal that he could not even remember hearing a stimulating idea from a Catholic pulpit? Kenneth Woodward, religion editor for *Newsweek*, was quoted in *Catholic Home*. He confided (April 1967) that he wished every diocese would print in its weekly paper copies of sermons delivered in local churches "to show how absurd and horrible most sermons are today."

And nobody wants a book of sermons. Not the publishers. When I first moved to New York in the early 1960s I visited with an editor of Harper and Row. They, along with Abingdon and Westminster, have probably put out more such books than any other publisher. When I offered some sermons for publication, the editor gave me a sad smile and said, "No one wants books of sermons. They don't sell. They are a drag. Can you come up with something else? Something else is what makes the print. 'How to' books are big. But not how to publish a book of sermons. You have perhaps even observed that some preachers disguise their sermons in meditations, and 'thoughts,' and little story collections. Anything sells but don't call them sermons."

After all this crepe-hanging funeral dirge for the pulpit, which is related to the local parish, let us lift up our eyes to the hills, from whence cometh our help. The university campus. Across the land the college chapel and university pulpit continue to impress me with their cutting edge, excitement, and contagious stimulation.

You note by now that I have not brought out the Number One Example of Preaching in America Today. You noticed that. Do you know why? And do you know why I have lifted up the college pulpit and university chapel over him and the local parish? Because they, on the firing line of the campus, deal with fire instead of talking about it.

They experience conversion instead of describing it. They preach in the trenches and not from the comfortable distance of studio and TV set. I mean, if preaching is relevant and the gospel a saving experience, it is going to be all worked up over war and peace and civil rights and poverty. It will bloody its nose in Watts or Harlem, scuffle with the rulers of this present darkness, and do the hard thinking and harder speaking to a people who thirst after truth and righteousness and believe that God meets them where they are but not always as they are.

My heroes? Some are professors, preachers in disguise, others are scholars, speakers in work clothes. Some are churning around in the secular university power centers but they are constant and inspiring and nervy and that is what the Christian faith and the Christian life are all about.

The New Theologians and the Old Church

If we were to use World War II as the dividing line that signaled the change in much of the church's life, we should see that the influence and attention of theologians has been leaning toward the campus rather than the parish.

Historically the swing has been back and forth between the two. A trained clergy has always been at home on campus. A New Testament scholar finds the pulpit as challenging as the lecture hall. Luther spoke of himself as a poor parish priest. Yale was founded by the perseverance and vision of seven clergymen who knew the wider ministry of a university. Of course, the divinity school and seminary were usually part of the higher education strata and doctors of divinity gravitated to the training and schooling of ministerial students.

The goal was the parish. The key was the pulpit. The instrument was the open Bible and the effort of scholar and seminary was to prepare men for this ministry. A scattering of other possibilities were evident—missions, chaplaincies, and church-related college teaching posts. But the primary concentration has been to the preaching, pastoral ministry, and since World War II this has changed.

Very few young men now announce to their congregation, "I'm going to preach." Rather, they are heard to speak in terms of service to mankind, to Christ and the church. A considerable interest has grown in the whole field of counseling and clinical training. A young pastor in New York, when discussing his daily round of chores and responsibilities, does not speak of the hours spent in the library, study, or sermon-making shop—rather, he talks about his "counseling load" or the number of cases that he has each week.

Teaching comes in for wide discussion. So does the relationship with public and private welfare agencies, poverty programs, and youth activities. Preaching has taken a back seat, so far back that one would find it difficult to name the professors of preaching at half a dozen leading seminaries. Whereas, a quarter of a century ago, we quickly recall Halford E. Luccock at Yale,

Henry S. Coffin at Union, Charles W. Gilkey at Chicago, Clarke at Princeton, etc.

On March 19, 1967, the New York *Times* carried excerpts from a convocation address given by Robert M. Hutchins at the University of Chicago.

His topic and mood were sharply drawn. The culture of the Western world, particularly the United States, was under examination. He asked:

> Nor do we know whether prosperity and power are legitimate ends for a human society, and under present conditions we have no way of finding out. When all the social institutions that might sit in judgment on the spirit of the age, the church, the press, and the university, are out-shouting one another in the flattering chorus, what chance have we of learning what the spirit ought to be?

Is it foolish to believe that the spirit of God is one that must pervade our life and time? Then let us be foolish. St. Paul enlarges on this when he says that God gives us a spirit of wisdom and might, a spirit of power and understanding.

It is a current, unending problem. Continues Dr. Hutchins:

> What power can accomplish, the United States can do. What prosperity can give, the United States can enjoy. Power and prosperity are good things if you know what to do with them. At the moment, the United States is the most powerful, the most prosperous and the most dangerous country in the world.

Our people gag on a statement like that. They throw sand in the air and murmur in the aisles. And the most sickening, pitiful development is the failure of the religious community, known as the church, to offer any guidance, clarity, and judgment to a murmuring, rebellious people.

Church as Judge

Only the smallest segment of the American religious establishment has taken a consistent and steady stand on the war in Vietnam. As more soldiers pour into that embattled peninsula, it becomes quieter in the church social halls and sanctuaries. (When the American Catholic bishops were invited to be part of the Clergy Concerned about Vietnam and hold discussions in Washington, only eleven out of 250 even bothered to reply to the letter of invitation.)

Many, like Robert McAfee Brown, recall the urgency of Albert Camus, who had great hopes for the church and the kingdom of the Spirit and was anxious for it to say a good word for humanity.

> What the world expects of Christians is that Christians should speak out, loud and clear, and that they should voice their condemnation in such a way that never a doubt, never the slightest doubt, should rise in the simplest man. That they should get away from abstraction and confront the blood-stained face history has taken on today.

But the blood-stained face is someone else's color on our TV screen. It is someone else's country, someone else's boy, someone else's widow. When you walk through the large rail stations of our cities and you see the caskets quietly stacked on the shipping dock, you know that the war has come home again, shadowing another house and breaking hearts from here to Saigon.

Do mothers cry in Vietnam as well as Vermont? Are memorial services held for Black Pajamas as well as Green Berets? The Christian really has allegiance to God's whole world, and at pain of persecution and abandonment by nationalists and tunnel-vision patriots, must speak the word of reconciliation and peace—as unpopular and unwelcome as they sound.

The question is that—not, where is wisdom to be found and the price of understanding? No, where is nerve to be found and the price of raw courage?

It is not with the churches.

It is not with the National Association of Evangelicals. It does not reside with the National Council of Churches. The American bishops, Catholic or otherwise, have no comment to make.

The churches have nothing to say because they are panting under the loads and burdens of housekeeping projects. We live in the biggest buildings-and-grounds, construction-and-shrub-trimming period of Christian history. We have stained more glass and hung more drapes and gilded more crosses and plated more chalices than any era of Christendom.

Since 1951, the United Presbyterian Church has laid eight hundred million dollars on its local members for local projects. Like air conditioning and closed-circuit television and imported bell towers and carved pulpits and authentic hand-crafted pipe organs starting at $75,-000 per. And after all this fund raising, mortgaging, blueprinting, salesmanship, we wonder bug-eyed why the church not only has no time to discuss the wars of American contemporary history—be they on poverty or people—but why the church is also the solid seat of opposition to and criticism of those who would seek solutions and settlement.

If the American church was just a little jostled by the God is Dead movement, happening, or fad, then a partial truth may have popped out: that the God of love, justice, reconciliation, and judgment is dead to a large number of "believers" who have found a substitute. That the concern of those outside the church is accurate, that our culture, church, society, nation—what have you—is suffering from a malady that is spreading in epidemic forms.

Cried Hutchins:

> The danger that will threaten you in the next 25 years is sclerosis, of the imagination, the vision, the character, the mind, and the heart. This is a disease especially virulent in opulent countries . . .

We follow an order of service, and in most of our churches it has a prayer of confession. What do we confess? Where dare we to start, if honesty is served and truthfulness abounds? Strangely, it may lead us to a corporate sense of guilt and salvation as well as individual soul-winning. Here we part with Graham and most contemporary evangelism. We are going to rise or fall together, brethren. Check that out with your Hebrew background.

Rethinking Religion

How do you get people to think seriously about religion? How do you crack the marble-coated minds which have encased the free inquiry of so many "religious" people? Perhaps that was the greatest value of the God is Dead school of theology. This group of radical theologians jarred the complacency of the religious scene for more than a year.

Again, Albert Outler puts the sequence in order when he wrote in *Who Trusts in God:*

> Taken by itself, the "death of God" was a relatively brief episode. Already its excitements have faded. But it was a landmark for our time because it exposed as nothing else had done before it the disorderly hodge-podge of belief, misbelief, and disbelief in the churches, the fading loyalties of many in mainstream Protestantism, and the haphazard fortunes of theological publicity. We know now what we only surmised before: that disbelief in traditional Christianity is now epidemic not merely among the intelligentsia but the literate masses as well.

Now it is all over. The public would be hard-pressed to name two or three of the professors and clergymen who made such a splash in saying that God is dead. However, those men did force millions to ask themselves in what way God was alive and working in their lives and in His world.

Once, hippies were the religious shockers. The serious hippies—not the poor runaway teen-agers—became an embarrassment and threat to the religious establishment. Their style of dress and mode of living seemed much closer to the poverty of the New Testament than the luxurious cathedrals of Fifth Avenue or the black limousines of the bishops.

Protests of the war, self-denial in ordinary comfort and conveniences, the looking after the lonely and the runaways seem to be pretty close to the saintly people found in the four Gospels.

Milton Himmelfarb, an executive of the American Jewish Committee, offered this comment on the approach taken by the Flower People:

> What is new . . . and unfamiliar is the hippies' thirst for spirituality, for religion . . . for a wholeness of experience. . . . They are not saying that religion or spirituality or even that horrible word, mysticism, are a lot of baloney. They are saying that they respect those things and may even want to have them for themselves.

In this respect, the beard-and-sandal group is in much more tension with the religious establishment than, say, the cashmere-sweater, color-television crowd. For those who represent the church are measured against a standard which is there for the whole world to read: the Bible. There it is—the plans, guidelines, and standards of the Christian life. The hippie starts reading scripture aloud and sensitive souls within the church begin to blush.

It would not surprise me at all to have historians write a hundred years from now that the hippie movement in America was one of the primary reasons for the church's re-examination of its own goals and concerns in the world's most affluent society. As they say, J.C. is for us!

The Underground Church

If you want an "in" topic these days, you talk about the underground church. It will be discovered soon by radio talk shows and the scholarly television panels. Articles will flourish in the weekly news magazines. Learned and not so learned speakers will be in hot demand to inform the public about the latest happening in religion.

Underground movements are either violent or gentle reactions against established institutions. They may be political-military groupings which extend their resistance to a hostile government long after a truce has been signed —such as the "underground" in France during the German occupation in World War II. Spain, Ireland, Mexico have lived with such revolutionary elements in this century and others may erupt in unexpected places in South America.

The underground railway was an effective and active organization to assist runaway slaves just prior to the Civil War. Stretching from Dixie to the Canadian border, it was supported by devout and caring people who could no longer accept slavery and the cultural accommodations that the public had made.

Underground movies are flourishing in many of our cities . . . some in reaction to the fixed codes that have governed Hollywood and the film industry, others to satisfy perverted minds and indulgent habits of wealthy patrons who call it art.

The underground church reaches far into the history of religion, recruiting sensitive souls who were spiritually starved by the provisions offered by temple, synagogue, or church. Nicodemus is a prominent example of this spiritual torment: he was an official of the religious establishment that was hostile to Jesus, yet personally drawn to this man from Nazareth. He sought instruction from Jesus at night, and by so doing, joined the religious underground.

Dietrich Bonhoeffer was one of the most vital personalities in the underground church of Nazi Germany. His projects were so clever and his leadership so cunning that he operated an entire seminary "underground," moving his students from city to town whenever discovery seemed imminent. Because Bonhoeffer had gone underground, the entire generation of postwar clergymen was influenced and shaped by his writing and witness.

Right now there is an underground church in the United States. There are no officers, mailing lists, conventions, or handbooks. Don't look for a calendar of events, an annual budget, or a women's auxiliary. No choirs or building drives. Just the quiet, informal, even infrequent, meeting of people who want to serve the God who is the source of all love and justice. There may be discussion, Bible study, small group worship in somebody's house or apartment. Denominational lines, racial differences have vanished.

The underground church is most visible when it surfaces on community and national social issues. The "members" are present for the peace demonstrations, an interfaith dialogue, a discussion with the city council over fair housing or open-housing ordinances. Always it seems to be people trying to love and serve God in the drama, delight, and distress of the world. Right now they count the institutional church as dead. But by their faith they are saying that God is alive.

Obedience or Disobedience?

When a national dream turns sour, when dissension and unhappiness pervade society, when current events take shocking turns, some people seek a simple answer.

So it was that Richard Nixon wrote in the October 1967 *Reader's Digest:*

> Our teachers, preachers, and politicians have gone too far in advocating the idea that each individual should determine what laws are good and what laws are bad, and that he then should obey the law he likes and disobey the law he dislikes.

Nixon thereby suggests that the 300,000 clergymen in these United States are in part responsible for the general moral collapse of the body politic and could be specifically charged with the burning of Newark, Watts, and Detroit, our poor showing in Vietnam, and the existence of third-generation families on welfare.

Since Nixon names no clergymen, teachers, or politicians, he tries to succeed with this villain-seeking piece by accusing an entire professional group in this country.

The premise of his text is that you ought to obey unjust laws.

According to Nixon's stance, Moses had no right or moral basis for his breaking out of Egypt. He should have obeyed the laws of Pharaoh (wicked, unjust, and oppressive) and relieved the slavery of his people through patience and trust in Nile justice. Exodus is really a primer on civil disobedience and one man's willingness to follow the dictates of God in preference to the threats and rewards of the delta society.

Any study of the life of Jesus Christ reveals One who put his face against the prevailing order of the church and state and taught a higher and more demanding law—The Kingdom of Heaven. His followers saw the inside of prison and arena because they chose to obey God and disregard the restrictions of wicked laws and perverted judges.

Do you know how many years chattel slavery was the law, enforced by armies, administered by kings and governments, and accepted by populations? We had 3,000 years of it until the people no longer could stomach this "lawful order" and threw it up. There was plenty of gentle and violent civil disobedience in the process, for the longer an unjust law, the more violent the change.

What Nixon and his counselors need to understand is this: our society is going through torment in the streets, violence in the ghettos, demonstrations in the universities, and picketing in the plazas because people want change.

Basically it is a search for more love, more justice, more humanity, and more dignity. If it were already a wonderful reality, we would have more picnics and fewer protests.

And where is the clergy in all this? What the clergy is really teaching is obedience—obedience to the demands, expectations, and requirements of a just and holy God, as they see them. When that feeling of allegiance and loyalty takes hold of people, they can no longer live with injustice and wickedness.

In our worry over the role of the clergy and our apprehension over some of the leadership that has such a firm grip on the Christian church, it is heartening to notice some events that surprise and delight.

Retire to Do God's Will

Paul Emile Cardinal Leger, archbishop of Montreal, shook up the religious world when he announced his resignation from one of the world's largest dioceses. Beginning in early 1968, he became a "simple priest" working among African lepers.

What is refreshing and surprising is the willingness of a sixty-three-year-old cleric to make such a radical and sweeping change in his ministry. To begin a new work after forty is hardly the advice of secular personnel officers.

Fortunately, history is engraved with the lives of men and women who made dramatic moves when others their age were talking retirement plans and South Seas cruises.

From the Old Testament we learn that Moses was forty before he came to grips with the moral question of ghetto life under the Egyptian sky. His well-to-do friends were probably buying winter homes along the Mediterranean while he was contemplating a Red Sea Revolution. Strange, unpredictable—but necessary for the spiritual advance of society are these men over forty.

When the British decided to march on Lexington and destroy the arms and munitions of the colonists, you would almost anticipate the thrilling night ride of twenty-two-year-old Paul Revere. Not so! Revere was a graying silversmith of forty who discovered that new perils and opportunities come at middle age as well as in the teens.

Frank Lloyd Wright did not receive wide recognition until he was nearly fifty and achieved some of his most brilliant architectural achievements in his mid-eighties. The creative spirit really observes no birthday boundary—and some of the most dynamic lives don't seem to get fired until the first four decades are invested.

What jarred many people about the resignation of Cardinal Leger is not that he was leaving a powerful, comfortable position in the Catholic Church, but his succinct reasons for such a decisive move. A careful reading shows that his analysis applies to every man who has made his peace with a troubled and raging world:

> I have reached the age where a certain sclerosis of soul and body might set in. The spur must be used to get out of the rut. It is so easy to become installed in comfortable habits after having exercised authority for a long time, especially in a diocese where Catholics comprise the large majority.

My hope is that the over-forty, over-fifty crowd will examine more carefully their commitment to the bridge club, the golf cart, and the Palm Springs tan. There are thousands of people who need to take personally Cardinal Leger's searching appeal for a more sensitive and compassionate existence:

> The church is essentially a missionary body. The day when she ceases to go toward those who have not yet received the Gospel, she willl have turned in on herself and will have been unfaithful to her mission. But if the Gospel must be proclaimed to all men, it is directed first to all the humble, to the poor in spirit for whom our Lord always showed a particular concern.

Is it possible for members of an affluent society to respond to the dictates of the Christian faith? The answer may come in the lives of those who retire in order to do God's will!

«4»

The New Layman

No matter how you shade it, the image of the layman in the eyes of the church has always been that man or woman who took seriously the duties, regulations, and forms as prescribed by ecclesiastical authority. Those limits and boundaries have widened to a remarkable degree. The range of activity has been spirited and, at times, wildly imaginative. But always it has been held within the order and discipline of the church and that practically means under the thumb of the clergy. Or the bishop, or the Conference or Presbytery or Diocese or Convention.

You may add terms and enlarge the definitions but the final rein of power and control has been clerical.

The most careful limiting of the laity has been possible through the church's teachings of holiness. Over the centuries the focus of holiness has been in the handling of the sacraments and the clergy had the power to offer or refuse the functions that made the experience available. One was indeed "admitted" to the Lord's Table. He's also, under the regulations of discipline of every church, able to suffer excommunication from the Lord's Table and be denied the services and benefits of the clergy. If he wanted to get married or buried, the church controlled the access to the altar or the graveyard. They presumably would swing wide or slam the gates of the Kingdom of Heaven. Holiness has been understood to be the temple and the cathedral door has an inside lock.

In times past the temple/cathedral had to secure living quarters for its priests and ministers, aides and attendants. Schools were erected to provide the education and training of these staffs. Vast libraries were necessary and sprawling grounds accompanied the increase of faculty and students. Enormous farmlands, productive agrarian enterprises, and substantial work crews were vital to the functioning of the temple.

Hospitals and orphanages were established to aid the poor and deprived. Colleges and universities, teaching orders and scribes, printers and publishers, all became part of the growing enterprise which marked the establishment church, visible and powerful in the world. The laymen were there to worship and assist, to contribute and support the life of the religious community, and to find their way to holiness, which was understood in the way proscribed by the clergy.

It is not surprising that the fondest layman was one who fulfilled the highest expectations of the clergy. His generous financial gifts, his unlimited energy and concern for churchly matters, his loyalty and affection in the goals of the sacred community were recognized and rewarded. To be a layman was to be a churchman. And a churchman pursued as far as possible the life of holiness that was allowed him by the clergy. For, after all, he could go only so far. The highest holiness was ordination and should he accomplish that, he would no longer be a layman, would he!

The formality of religion has always sought to separate the sacred from the secular, the pious from the profane. It is a constant chore of ecclesiastical surveillance. It requires a knowledge of the law and a brutal, unceasing maintenance without deviation or dissent. Can we at all imagine the volcanic eruptions that John the Baptist created with his holiness in the wilderness, his ethics in the desert, his salvation under the sky and in the rushing waters of the Jordan, instead of the hushing murmurs of the sanctuary?

John the Baptist was a layman! He scorned the religious guidelines of the spiritual Pentagon in Jerusalem. God's love and justice were a reality to be experienced in the affairs of men and nations. Forgiveness was not a prayer of pardon in the temple, but an act of contrition in the counting house.

Rise and Decline of Lay Leadership

I'm not at all sure about the reasons for the rise and decline of lay leadership in the world. Do the creative spirits withdraw quietly from the institutional church when it hugs too closely and affectionately the status quo? Almost every rise of the institutional religious organization is accompanied by popular support of the lay people. Yet over the centuries, when the church becomes complacent, fat, rich, and arrogant, and when you look a little closer, the pews no longer hold the bright and thoughtful people who are the church, too.

In his powerful little book, *The Vision of God,* Kenneth E. Kirk provided a partial answer to our question. On the theological-intellectual basis he quoted Father Pourrant, who claimed:

> "In the patristic period, no books of devotion were composed for the Christians living 'in the world.' The same is true of a great part of the middle ages. . . . There were not two 'spiritual lives,' one for the ascetic, the other for ordinary Christians. There was only one; and that was monastic. From the birth of monasticism, Christians who proposed to take the quest for perfection seriously became monks—either by retiring to the desert or cloister, or by practising domestic asceticism of the monastic kind. . . . Hence it is not surprising that spiritual writers should never have thought of addressing themselves to secular Christians; nor that their piety was monastic in character."

Observed Kirk in his studies of the life of the faith:

> So grew up the extraordinary perplexing phenomenon of a double moral standard in Catholicism—a lower and a higher grade of Christian achievement—the distinction between counsels and precepts, the religious and the secular vocations, the contemplative and active lives. There can be no doubt that the distinction saved Christianity. . . . But it left the Christian moralist with the curiously elusive problem— How far, if at all, is the distinction thus expressed of any ultimate validity?

I believe that Jesus and John the Baptist, his forerunner, gave the answer to that theological dilemma. Their pursuit of holiness and Godliness in the world brought them into unbearable conflict with the forces of church and state. John was beheaded. Jesus was crucified, and their deaths and the persecution of the disciples often grew out of raw struggles between laity and clergy.

Historically we have not wanted to admit that theme. Liberal clergymen have always angered conservative laymen, and conservative churchmen have infuriated liberal laymen. It is much deeper than this: the division rests on who really is understanding and pursuing the basic tenets of the Christian life. Where is justice to be found and who is the true champion of religious expression and human freedom? As Abbe Piré has put it:

> What matters today is not the difference between believers and nonbelievers, but that between those who care and those who do not care.

True to Himself

The new layman and his growing breed are those who quickly set their face against the church when it stops caring, stifles life, thwarts love, and perverts justice. To be true to the Kingdom, he is willing, painfully, to be the church's most virulent opponent and unceasing critic. To be a layman loyal to Jesus Christ is to tell it like it is. Holiness is creation. Righteousness is seeking God's handiwork. Discipleship is fulfilling one's greatest gifts to the glory of God, and working for the advancement of all men whom He has lovingly created. But love and justice have no obedience to the church. For the church was called to be their servant.

The style and shape of the new laity is hard to chart. How do we know what it will be like, since so much of the time requires a nerve and tenacity to improvise? It is one thing to say what shouldn't happen, but what about some suggestions for action?

We are helped by the past. In tracing the development of the biblical idea of God, Erich Fromm finds the essence of true religion to be the liberation of man.

> Not restriction or bind, but a development that enables him to acquire convictions and principles, and thus to be eventually "true to himself," rather than to be obedient to an authority.

If men are to be free and fulfill the image desired by God, they must challenge, confront, criticize all forms of human authority. Otherwise, Fromm sees only a serfdom, not salvation for men. The biblical idea of devotion to God and radical freedom are the survival tools that the new laity must seize if they are to be their own men.

> Full independence is one of the most difficult achievements; even if man overcomes his fixation to blood and soil, to mother and clan, he holds on to other powers that give him security and certainty: his nation, his social group, his family, or his achievements, his power, his money. Or he becomes so narcissistic that he does not feel a stranger in the world because he is the world, there is nothing besides him or outside him. . . . Independence is possible only if, and according to the degree to which, *man actively grasps the world, is related to it, and thus becomes one with it.*

And then Fromm puts his finger on the nerve when he concludes that

> . . . the beginning of liberation lies in man's capacity to suffer.

Israel experienced it in Egyptian slavery, in Babylonian captivity, in a longing and yearning to find the highest and fullest that God has promised. The Christian sees in the suffering of Christ a willingness to use even death on a Cross to fulfill the claims and call of God on all men. In suffering, conviction is formed, belief is shaped, and life given a dimension that separates the trivia from the truth.

Any person who sincerely pursues the Christian life

must expect that it holds the landmarks and detours of suffering. Far too often this has been a ghastly thought for the church to consider. When it is bent on saving its own soul, lands, power, prestige, influence, skin, it has little yearning for new Calvaries or another testing by fire. And it is possible to surround so thoroughly the life of believers with religious activities, planned pietism, calendared holidays, unbelievable financial burdens that the moral question need hardly be raised. Who has time to hear it?

We are helped by the past because the experience of the saints and seers of the Bible is also confirmed in the lonely adventures of men and women who believed and followed. In the last century we have some fascinating studies of the new laity who never apologized for their deviation from the norm, yet pursued it with good humor and frightening determination.

Lonely Hero of Labrador

When Wilfred Grenfell went to the snowy coasts of bleak Labrador he was hardly the champion of the religious establishment of Great Britain. Conservatives and fundamentalists were unsure of his theology. The medical societies had few to compare him with. Traditional churchmen were never entertained by his Sunday School pranks. The people loved him and I suspect that he was always his own man—at home or away.

When the large church conventions lionized his Labrador achievements and the international conferences vied for his appearances, he never wavered on the basics that he felt were to be overcome:

> The mistake about the use of the word faith is the worst mistake in the world. It makes young manhood despise faith. We mix up the use of faith with black coats, clerical collars, monkish gowns. We think of the life of faith as unnumbered religious services, convent or monastic practices, refraining from cards, theatres, wines, smoking, swearing, etc. We think of the "soul's awakening" as a desire to cross the hands on the chest, and turn up the eyes and carry a large book about, and probably wear a long gown like a Chinese woman's, ill adapted for easy movement and exceedingly undesirable. We think of the perfected life in heaven as encumbered with halos and white gowns and wings on our backs and our probable occupation as being eternal hymn-singing or harp-playing.

He was just getting warmed up with that opening.

> It seems impious to think of wearing rational dress, of baseball, of swimming, boating, or of doing anything else we really enjoy, in heaven. . . . How often I thought I would far sooner not be wakened out of my grave if I have to listen to everlasting harp-playing. I have looked at the goody-goody pictures, I have read the goody-goody books. I have hoped I would not have to lead a lamb about by a string.

Here was one of the great laymen of this hemisphere, trained as a physician, able to work with the young and the poor, loving sailing and the sea, and pouring out his life on the frozen coasts of Labrador. Or take the sunny isles of Samoa. There Robert Louis Stevenson culminated a life of travel and storytelling that indicates a pattern of existence which others might emulate.

From Scotland to Samoa

Stevenson came out of Edinburgh, Scotland, with a tubercular cough and a preparation in engineering and a degree in law. He quit both for a career in writing. He canoed through Belgium and France, saw California and hoped for health at Saranac Lake, New York. Along the way he gave the world *Treasure Island* and *Kidnapped* and *Dr. Jekyll and Mr. Hyde.*

His pursuit and longing for physical strength took him to the South Seas. I saw his tiny hut in Hawaii and the blue water he crossed to make his home at last in Samoa. It was here that he recorded his Vailima prayers, the daily petitions he offered for his household, and I imagine for all our homes:

> Lord, behold our family here assembled. We thank Thee for this place in which we dwell; for the love that unites us, for the peace accorded us this day, for the hope with which we expect the morrow, for the health, the work, the food, and the bright skies that make our lives delightful; for our friends in all parts of the earth, and our friendly helpers in this foreign isle.
>
> Let peace abound in our small company. Purge out of every heart lurking grudge. Give us grace and strength to forbear and to persevere.

Give us courage and gaiety and the quiet mind. Bless us, if it may be, in all our innocent endeavors.

And if it may not, give us strength to encounter that which is to come, that we be brave in peril, constant in tribulation, temperate in wrath, and in all changes of fortune and down to the gates of death, loyal and loving to one another.

As the clay to the potter, as the windmill to the wind, as the children to their sire, we beseech Thee of this help and mercy, for Christ's sake. Amen.

Stevenson lived almost five years—his last five—in the Samoan dispute between the British and the tribes of the island. These were tense times for a man in search of solitude and peace, yet he gave much of his flagging strength to the promotion of amity among the people of this distressed island.

In his last days he saw the start of a new road to his home that was built personally by the Samoans. These people developed and finished the road as an expression of their thankfulness to the teller of tales who had done so much to assist them in their trials.

He was deeply and profoundly moved by this gesture, and perhaps even more by the name they gave this highway; they called it *The Road of the Loving Heart.* What the world is crying out for is some more men and women of unique and wondrous talents to light dark paths, to tell great stories, and to be, in good season and bad, "brave in peril, constant in tribulation, temperate in wrath."

The Christian Folk Hero

Certain laymen have almost become folk heroes in the eyes of the Christian community—or at least that section which has had a burning missionary zeal for those in other lands who "have not heard the Gospel."

The anecdotes, adventures, and achievements of these overseas personalities may have been extended beyond the limits of verification. Others may have done mighty but unsung accomplishments. David Livingstone was orbited into popularity by the press as much as by the pulpit.

It was helpful, then, to have the research in the published biography of David Livingstone by Jack Simmons, who uncovered some startling material about his early life. Livingstone, it seems, was thinking of a call to foreign missionary service in his high-school days. In planning his strategy he concluded that he did not want to go only in the capacity of a speaker and preacher, so he prepared himself in the field of medicine as well as theology.

However, before even this essential preparation was completed, David Livingstone worked in a Glasgow, Scotland, mill, six days a week, allowing two hours in the evening for class work! He stayed with this demanding schedule for thirteen years and never faltered in the goal he set before himself.

Livingstone, indeed, made a massive impact on the African community with a frontal attack on the slave trade and through medicine and exploration. But as author Simmons indicates, he won the hearts of thousands of people because so many of his own years in preparation were identified with struggling laboring people. One of his most significant contributions to one particular tribe came about through his teaching starving farmers how to nourish their crops with irrigation ditches!

It is against such historic giants that the new layman must measure his goals and opportunities. There is no formula, outline, or manual for contemporary Christian witness. God moves among men with the gifts of talent, insight, motivation, compassion, and a fury for justice. In one life we may see a burst of artistic expression, in another scholarly perseverance. In some we find a distinct managerial ability, for a few a piercing understanding of social events.

But all believers—all who would attach themselves to the company of Jesus Christ—should have days of expectation and accomplishment. Especially in this world washed with bad news, war imminent, and the cynical "swinger" the idol of the jet set.

Against the World

But more than this, we are surrounded by a world of people, many of whom are governed only by their wants and desires and pleasures. Their attitudes are a constant battering against the personality of any person who wants to express the love of God. Many worldly types reject this, the love of God—they oppose it and necessarily would destroy it or else they will be converted by it.

A perfect example of this was described by the Associated Press at the Indianapolis Speedway one Memorial Day. Many of you recall the collapse of that aluminum grandstand where seventy people had been sitting, prepared for the beginning of the 500-mile race.

People had rented these makeshift seats for a good view of the race. Just before the beginning of the contest, the great aluminum structure swayed and smashed to the ground. Two men died with broken necks, sixty-eight were taken to hospitals with critical injuries. And then this poignant quote by one man standing next to the mass of struggling humanity:

> We went right back in and tried to lift up the scaffold. A man had the ashen look of death on his face. People not ten feet on either side of this thing were only interested in the race and not the screams and the moans. . . . Witnesses told of trying desperately to rescue the injured from under the pipes, while others on the ground went on drinking beer and munching fried chicken.

In these days of the electric generation described by Marshall McLuhan, in the mood of a culture that becomes restless when the game kickoff is delayed three minutes, when tempers flare at an intersection traffic light that "holds" too long, in an entertainment culture where a mature audience roars its abuse at the unfocused film on a theater screen . . . against this temperament it may become a sparkling Christian virtue to be a man or woman of patience. Not of the hour or day—but years.

Our instant frozen dinners, our immediate warm-up on the television set, our direct-distance dialing would not seem to encourage the pursuit of long-term, uncertain claims to success. But then, does not the Christian trust God to be in the Land of Time Enough, if the time is His and we are His people?

Douglas Steere, the great Quaker leader and philosopher, points to this condition in the work of one of his associates:

> The late Clarence Pickett tells movingly of his accepting invitations to visit Russian embassy parties in the '50's when he was almost the only non-Communist sympathizer there. "I was invited to the embassy parties in Washington and practically always made it a point to go. . . . I was looking to the time when we might have normal relations . . . when there would be people going back and forth between our two countries."

How trying, painful, exasperating are some of the tasks that Christians face to implement the gospel of love in a mocking world.

The prisoner, the prostitute, and the poor are not those who will be rehabilitated by a government bureau or an ecclesiastical conference. In each instance there must be someone or some group that is going to give their life to reclaim and restore those who are broken by sin and circumstance. On some occasions it may be aid and comfort to those we know. In many more it is directed to the stranger, the traveler, the victim who shares our day and places a claim upon our lives.

Alas, the growing organizational church has become a convenient wall between the Christian and the pangs of the world. We spell out the need in denominationally approved terms and then solicit support while at the same time trying to co-ordinate the resources of millions of people. Yet how easy it has been to leave it there. The tough and elusive human hangups can be ignored if the church or its leaders don't want to get their hands dirty or don't feel adequate to make a "meaningful response."

«5»

Anything, So Long As It's Secular

One of the difficult tasks of the Christian in contemporary culture is to sort out the valid, distinctive "happenings" that give meaning and depth, and, at times, entertaining diversion to a mass society.

The combination of forces that make up mass media have such an explosive effect on world culture that overnight the movies, television, and national weekly magazines can establish a personality or group, writer or school of thought, as an exhilarating fad or continuing idol. Or create national mourning.

"The assassination of President John F. Kennedy,"

wrote Henry Hews (*Saturday Review*, March 11, 1967), "is to most of us a sacred tragedy. A man who had come to symbolize a youthful, fresh, and idealistic approach to politics was cruelly erased from an era in which he was the most hopeful figure."

This really was shared deeply by the Protestant clergy, as well as by the Roman Catholic and Jewish communities. In fact, it is my belief that the switch within the ranks of the Protestant clergy from Nixon to Kennedy in the election of 1960, a switch which happened in about three weeks' time before November, may well have been the deciding factor in the victory of the young Irishman from Massachusetts. I think clergymen especially liked his self-effacing humor, his forceful speaking, and his candor in answering theological questions. At least one compilation of prayers, sermons, and memorial services offered in tribute to the young President from Hyannis Port has been published.

Some Blasphemous Absurdities

Yet this tragic national event became for some an excessive absurdity. Theologians seized this secular event in the life of the body politic and draped it with near-blasphemous tributes. Two able theologians, Donald E. Miller and Graydon F. Snyder, invited readers to look "at some of the crucial themes in the scriptural account of Christ's death and then see how they are illuminated by the spontaneous feelings and interpretations that the death of President Kennedy elicited."

The writers, I should add, quickly disclaimed any

desire to make Kennedy a "savior-king." Some of the comparisons they proposed to the ministry of Jesus and the administration of John F. Kennedy were startling to say the least, if not questionable.

> *"One has died for all; therefore all have died"* (2 Corinthians 5:14) . . . Not only Americans, but men of all nations have radically participated in the death of President Kennedy . . . "A piece of each of us died at that moment." (Senator Mike Mansfield.)
>
> *"Christ Jesus . . . did not count equality with God a thing to be grasped, but emptied himself . . ."* (Philippians 2:6–7). With this, Paul and the early church confess the voluntary nature of God's action in Jesus Christ. Whatever the motives of John F. Kennedy in seeking the office of President, one cannot help but notice the sign of dedication and service . . . "He had money, a beautiful wife, fine children, everything all the rest of us want. He didn't have to take our troubles on himself, but he did." (Unidentified Chicago house painter.)
>
> *"He set his face to go to Jerusalem"* (Luke 9:51). The gospel makes clear the resolute act of Jesus to go to Jerusalem and personally face his critics. The cross resulted from a deliberate act of Jesus to reconcile the Jewish nation by giving himself to them freely. Surely one of the major reasons for the trip to Dallas was the reconciliation of political differences. [There is where the danger begins for the theologian who pursues a parallel between Jesus and secular political leaders like Kennedy or Lincoln or whoever.]
>
> *"Rabbi, the Jews were but now seeking to stone you, and are you going there again?"* (John 11:8) . . . Kennedy did not have to go to Dallas and indeed was warned not to go.

Then the analogy presses into absurdity with this comparison:

> "*Your king is coming to you, humble and mounted on an ass*" (Matthew 21:5). The Christological motif of the gospel is that, though a man of power, Jesus came unarmed and unprotected. His openness was in itself a means of reconciliation. . . . [The authors applaud the fact that JFK entered a hostile city and did not take all the precautionary measures he could have.] As a sign of his confidence and as a symbol of reconciliation he came "*without the bubble.*" [italics theirs]

The authors, in the remainder of their dangerous essay, indicate that Kennedy's death, like that of Christ, effected reconciliation. How? "In the cortege there was no Jew, Catholic, or Protestant; no black or white, and the bear and the eagle sat down together. (The Russian ambassador said his people were 'deeply moved.')"

Without pressing this unfortunate analogy any further (and readily confessing to Kennedy's picture in the tents of the Arabs and the apartments of Puerto Ricans), I think such material stands as the awful dilemma facing those who wish to draw Christian conclusions from secular events. It is a theological exercise that borders on blasphemy or heresy and surely causes serious embarrassment to the Kennedy family.

Unfortunately, the most serious calamities usually happen to those who are identified most strongly with the Christian community. Rarely is it the nonbeliever or outsider who makes grand proclamations or improvisations on scripture and doctrine. And the injury is to the community, not to the puzzled outsider.

Jeane Dixon, who carries extraordinary credentials for prophecy, is a vital member of the Roman Catholic Church. Yet her reputation for daily attendance at Mass does not make it easier for her friends to believe her every utterance, prophecy, and prognosis of the human condition. She told the Writer's Club of Washington, D.C.:

> God made the world ONE on the day Kennedy died.

Here again we're not sure if God, Kennedy, or Jesus Christ have not been confused in the public mind by such a sweeping statement.

The Kennedy image has extended long past the tragic death of a winsome President. The Kennedy aura is indeed larger than life. The adventures, trials, hurts, and victories of almost any member of the large political family are more than our most aggressive tabloids can keep up with. One gives up counting the covers that decorate the weekly and monthly magazines with pictures of a Kennedy skiing or mountain climbing or sailing or dancing or riding horseback or walking John John. The fantasy of the public is fed by their mysterious movements, exotic journeys, and harrowing escapes. Those with small, uneventful lives attempt to make unfulfilled dreams come true when they chart the fun and games and political gambols of our stars from Hyannis Port.

James Bond: Man of the Decade

The mass media found perfect ingredients in the exploits of James Bond, 007 secret agent created by Ian Fleming. Here was the mixture of a handsome, single, well-dressed, rightly tailored, shoulder-holstered champion of the Cold War.

Bond became the man of the decade, moving freely in the maze of subtleties that had been spun in international intrigue. His sexual adventures became as routine as his escapes from hired assassins. Master of technological equipment, the scuba, the rocket, the hydrofoil, and the atom became his servants.

The public sucked up this diet with the emotion of starving elephants. In less than a decade, the James Bond bookshelf reached a sales of more than forty million copies and the movies, probably three times that number when you count the overseas audience.

Such an avalanche of sex, sport, and secret agentry went hardly unnoticed. Youngsters sported James Bond code books, identification cards, and telescopic rifles. Night-club entertainers titillated the audience with questions about Bond's girl friends and their strange names. The general public accepted without complaint the notion that the enemies of the world (Dr. No, Odd Job) were properly cast as Orientals. Evil, always black; Bond, white; and the girls, tan.

This little episode of Bond mania lasted at least four good years, not counting the first appearance of the earliest books. The sprawling, violent sexual abuses, the homosexual, lesbian themes, the subhuman categorization of Eastern peoples, the license, rather, necessity to kill, all this stormed across the public squares of the Western world with hardly the slightest throat-clearing from the Christian community.

On the contrary, John Knox Press, a Southern Presbyterian publishing house came forward with *The Devil with James Bond.* This book extolled the virtues of Bond and proposed almost a secular sainthood for this leering young man on the flying striptease.

The author certainly warned us what to expect from this bizarre interpretation of secular sainthood:

> But suddenly out of the swirling mists of contemporary ambiguity regarding the nature and worth of mankind, a mysterious figure has appeared. Is he a modern Perseus armed by the gods in order to slay Medusa? St. George on a white horse on his way to kill a dragon? Don Quixote in search of windmills? Christian of *Pilgrim's Progress* traveling through the Slough of Despond or imprisoned in the castle of Giant Despair?
>
> No, none of these exactly, but a figure uniquely appropriate to the modern idiom: Commander James Bond, the incredible British undercover agent 007. . . .

With that shovelful, Mrs. Ann Boyd digs us a deeper trench by recalling the "weird coincidence" that the fourth movie in the Ian Fleming package, *Thunderball,* hit the theaters in New York—hold steady for this—on December 21, 1965. Why is that so jarring? The winter solstice, that's why! Because that cold, wintry, snow-blowing night a goodly number of citizens pulled away from the holy preparations of Christmas and Chanukah for deeper primordial reasons:

> Suddenly this latest mass-media symbol had zeroed in on the night on which in ancient times the first story-tellers were compelled by the terrors of primitive man to form images of hero figures who rescue the day from the terrors of the winter night!

This, I hope, is preparation for the rightful place that the author is about to give James Bond in history and saga. With Tarzan or Superman? Please.

> The figure of Bond consequently joins a long rank of mythological and literary figures who have served as symbols of transformation at various times of cultural crises in the Western world . . . within secular writings such a list of heroes would include the figures of Perseus, Hercules, Hiawatha, Beowulf, Rustam of Persia, and Christian of *Pilgrim's Progress,* to name only a few.

The author then seems to search further for confirmation of the James Bond deliverer role, and so adds:

> Within the Old Testament and Apocrypha there are stories of David fighting Goliath and Daniel conniving against Bel and the dragon. In the New Testament, the book of Mark is full of stories of Jesus casting out demons. . . .

Needless to say, there are massive booby traps strung for the glib adventurers who seek to extract religious and ethical relevance from the folk heroes of a vulgar culture. In our yearning to be "in," as one writer described it, to find a handle, we may succeed in springing a trap door that opens into pure empty froth.

The Professional Approach to the Secular

As the Christian community scans the horizon for a new style and approach to the secular, it may want to stand aside at times and watch the professionals who make a living at it. It seems that we often are so desirous of being accepted as part of the television or movie or literary or show-biz or record-pressing scene that we flop over the boundaries of good sense and good taste.

I mean, we want our clothes to have just the right cut; our jokes to be the funniest, and too often, the dirtiest; our buildings and appointments, *so tasteful;* our benefits, the biggest; and our music, the loudest. But it doesn't often come off. And what we have to give in the world comes not by competing with its sophistication, but by refining it. Not by chasing its secularity, but by harnessing it. Not by praising its worldliness, but by pondering it. And when we think we are the most safe, the trap is sprung, the railing collapses, the landmarks vanish.

And it may seem harsh to imply that some promoters are so greedy for the popular wave that catches the public fancy that they create books on the Christian and Anything, if Anything is Secular and is selling big in Madison Avenue, the funny papers, or the late movies. (John Knox Press put out an expensive promotion piece for their Bond book, complete with James Bond brief case, accessories, and display kit, that tickled the fancy of all booksellers—religious or otherwise.)

So the Christian community faces the twin peril of being in the world and of it, without clarity, distinction, or perception, and being out of it and not with it—ignoring the opportunities and findings and rewards of the secular because we are afraid of the stain, and at times, the shame.

The resurgency of nihilism and the continued dominance of a Theater of the Absurd have been more treachery than treasure for the participants from the Christian camp. Certain novelists and playwrights have appealed to those who are followed as critics in the established church. Too frequently it seems that a critic announces: I am a Christian. I like this book. Therefore, this book is Christian. It may be pure junk, a joke on the public, shockingly foul, but we must praise it as inherently soaked with truth, especially if all these things are present. I disagree.

Some esteemed critics can be just as wrong or right as the next guy in the car pool. When Senator Fulbright criticized President Johnson for not being more explicit about the early bombing pause in Vietnam, his wife met him at home and said something that no senator, reporter, or public figure thought of: "Can't you ever keep your mouth shut!"

Miracle of the Rose

When Jean Genet, the French author, produced *Miracle of the Rose,* the Reverend Tom Driver of Union

Seminary reviewed it with such high praise that you thought it was the greatest thing since sliced bread. It is a major achievement of modern literature. "The world we enter here is that of delinquents, homosexuals, pimps, burglars, and murderers. The reader may regard them as unfortunates or riffraff; in Genet's eyes, and in each others', they are heroes and the attendants of heroes." As we are led on into Driver's review of this foolish life and filthy setting, the rules are slyly changed, values distorted, and love perverted.

What is pathetic and sickening is the fascination that some literary clubs have for the perverted mind and twisted souls of this world. If the setting is an institution of demented people, a prison with homosexual marriages and murders, high points are given for such bizarre and shocking charades. Some Christian leaders think this is a good thing: dig up lots of dirt, profanity, sexual perversions because this is how life is. Well, that may be how some people's lives are led—the queer world, the sadistic plunderers, the addicts and the thieves and the whores have been around since the first sunlight. But the big point that has to be cleared is this: the Christian community has always greeted these dropouts from society in the expectations of change and conversion, and offers forgiveness and reconciliation. The present trend of some writers seems to be to let them glory in their filth because then they can tell it like it is. For, as Driver adds, "Sordid as all this is, *Miracle of the Rose* is not a dirty book"! Of course not. "The novel traces a biographical change in Genet from passive and feminine behavior to 'masculine homosexual love.'" As if that wasn't enough of a conversion experience, Driver suggests that Genet "transforms experiences of degradation into spiritual exercises and hoodlums into bearers of the majesty of love. Imagination is to Genet what prayer is to the man of God."

To the Highest Heaven

I think that we must be sure of one thing. The Christian community in most of its glistening moments has always been able to take those who had suffered the worst shame, perversion, and depravity and lift them up to the highest heaven of hope and recovery. St. Paul, in the letter to Titus, had a few Jean Genets in view when he wrote:

> Be ready for any honest work, to speak evil of no one, to avoid quarreling, to be gentle, and to show perfect courtesy toward all men. For we ourselves were once foolish, disobedient, led astray, slaves to various passions and pleasures, passing our days in malice and envy, hated by men and hating one another.

Life was ghastly. Prostitution in the Greek temples was a re-enactment of everything Genet ever imagined, all in the name of religion. Slavery was constant. Death was daily. And in this beastly, turbulent culture the first band of Christians dared to offer a few words of comfort and aid. So foolish, so funny. Trying to be clean in mind and body. Talking about Jesus as if he had never been strung up. Nervy with magistrates. Solemn before soldiers. Helping others to carry out the trash, whether it was refuse from the mind or the manor. And those strange multi-racial, bilingual communities that began to flourish in Asia Minor converted one Jean Genet after another. How or why?

> When the goodness and loving kindness of God our Savior appeared, he saved us, not because of deeds done by us in righteousness, but in virture of his own mercy. (*Titus* 3:4–5)

When you get right down to the parking-lot level, the Christian life takes every horror story and gives it a new dimension of change and hope. If the gospel of Jesus Christ did that once, it will do it always.

For instance, one gallant reviewer of James Bond books for *Christianity Today* was quite intrigued with the valiant attempts of Miss Boyd and her beguiling analysis. A little further on in the review of Miss Boyd's book he admitted he had not read any of the Fleming series, so breathlessly went out and bought one!

Are we not saying that in too many instances the Christian community does not know where to praise and where to blast in secular affairs, in worldly films, in literary circles, in mass media, in cultural exchange? Harsh? I think not.

The most perceptive and immediate criticism of the vulgarity of Bond and the obscenity of the Matt Helm-Ann Margaret films came from the pens of Judith Crist and other secular writers.

The most vigorous and consistent complaints that I

heard personally about the Pussy Galore, Mary Kravzit characters on theater marquees were from those not associated with the church, but daily workers in show business and public relations. They didn't think it funny or contemporary or clever. Said one, "It was just dirty, Dad, and I don't know how you can ignore it."

«6»

The Message and the Men

The Christian church has certain responsibilities to its members as well as to the larger community in its discussion of international conflict or a racial struggle in the cities or the generation gap:

1. Of all the institutions and organizations in our society, it stands charged by its own creed with the highest responsibility for raising the moral question. This is not expected from the country club, the volunteer fire company, the den mothers or the Fairfield County Bird Watchers. But the church—yes. This must be done in and out of season, for the gospel of Christian life

is one concerned about peace, reconciliation, world community, human brotherhood, and international justice.

2. The Christian community joins hands with those of all religious, moral, and spiritual endeavors to challenge the goals of a warfare society. Historically, the church has a poor record. From Constantine until now, the church has blessed wars, consecrated Crusaders, baptized blitzes, and passed the ammunition. Arthur Moore has said that ever to ask the institutional church to speak in forceful, prophetic terms to a sick, decaying society is like asking a computer to sing a love song. Let it be acknowledged that as America is searching its conscience on Vietnam and war, the church is struggling for its own soul, the integrity of its message, and the courage of its convictions.
3. Since the Christian community—the church—must raise the moral question—not in falsetto tea-sipping tones, but in a ringing challenge to the presumptions of government and the established policies of this fantastically powerful nation (and any state, for that matter)—let it recognize the full meaning of dissent. Let it realize that it will be decorated with the wardrobe of anti-Americanism, that it will be plastered with the slogans of subversion, that it may well be smeared with the sarcasm of "patriots." To dissent in the comfort of a cathedral or classroom is one thing—to challenge the powerful structure of a nation is quite another.
4. Let those within the church who through reason of conviction, compassion, or compulsion seek to apply the requirements of their faith to the performance of their fatherland do so in good humor, in a dispensable self-righteousness, in listening as well as asking, being confident of one thing, that the search for Truth is no man's absolute province.

5. Let the climate of discussion and inquiry be open to certain general agreed ground rules:
   a. That as far as the Christian faith goes, its message and its gospel, its outreach, and its followers, that it knows no national boundaries, that it scorns human designations of race or color or political precinct. It believes that God's children are in Hanoi, Haifa, and Hot Springs, Arkansas.
   b. That the Christian community will not be part of the splintering up of God's people into sinful human terms, like Yellow Peril or Black Power or Chinese hordes or savages or whatever easily obtained slogan is employed to build hate and increase enmity.

In Houston, on October 27, 1967, Captain Eddie Rickenbacker said that

> . . . peace demonstrators are a bunch of bums. The U.S. should bomb the ports, dams, and population of North Vietnam. That's what airplanes are for. You're not fighting human beings over there—you're just fighting two-legged animals. The people are just slaves. That's all war is for is to kill and win, to destroy, to defeat the population of your enemy.

It's that kind of attitude and venom that the Christian community has to challenge and confront if it is going to give the gospel a cutting edge in this turbulent world.

For the Serious Players

The involvement of the church in the world means doing one's homework. Sunday afternoon statements about war and peace, Black Power, and housing and mortgage rates for minorities are going to be pure baloney without thoughtful, tireless study. It means the reading of long reports, scholarly essays, financial studies, and laboratory findings. Any meaningful thrust of the Christian message into the last half of the twentieth century is going to come from people who have a biblical concordance in one hand and a Standard and Poor's Stock Digest in the other. It means scanning the recommendations of the Space Center in Houston one day and reviewing surveys of air pollution the next.

Ralph Nader, in his auto safety and meat inspection reports, showed that nothing can be left to the "experts." Technicians and trained minds can provide facts, data, history, and strategy. But every human encounter is a moral one and the Christian needs to be alert and aggressive to guide and shape the choices.

Vietnam stands as a ghastly example of the question, "Where did we go wrong?" Forget blaming one party or one President or one session of Congress. Ignore, for the moment, the staggering profits made by certain industries who turned this calamity into the juiciest moneymaker ever. Hold back your questions about a military establishment that wanted to try out its new war toys in a limited conflict. Ask but one question and put it not to the White House, the Pentagon, or West Point, but to the church. Where was the church in all this deception and misdirection of the world's most powerful nation?

It took at least four years of active fighting for the religious community of America to begin to probe for some background, history, and understanding of what Vietnam was all about.

William Sloan Coffin, Jr., the chaplain of Yale, pleaded in the summer of 1965 for the churches of America and the membership represented to read just one book about Vietnam. Any book, any author—foreign or domestic, any title. Read something about the life of this people, its trying and bloody story. Its deceptions, sellouts, parceling, and intimidations.

Because of my position as book editor of the *Christian Herald,* it was my responsibility to read books on Vietnam. As of this writing, I have read two dozen such books and I believe that if the churches had launched even a half-hearted study program, the bombing might have stopped a year earlier, the military-scientific community might have been neutralized, and 30,000 caskets need not have been flown home.

Little questions that were terribly basic:

What was the nature of the conflict?

Surely the most superficial understanding of Vietnam would reveal the historic pride and self-determination of this Asiatic people.

Here is a culture with a recorded history of more than two thousand years!

Here is a community—divided, torn, and bleeding. Yet with a fierce pride, having wrestled a dominant Chinese neighbor and conqueror for more than a thousand years!

Bernard Fall told of the museums in Hanoi which proudly displayed the struggle of Vietnam in their contest with China for independence. They endured French domination for eighty years and Japanese occupation for five years. Should it seem so strange to this nation that the

American adventure in "democracy" appears to be yet another chapter in foreign intervention?

Where did the rest of Asia stand on the threat which we in America felt was so harrowing and urgent that we committed billions of dollars and hundreds of thousands of men?

Once, the President said he was going to call the roll of those who live in that part of the world, in the great arc of Asian and Pacific nations. Supporting allies.

So he called Thailand, Malaysia, Singapore, the Philippines, Australia, and New Zealand.

He did not name India, Pakistan, and Japan. He ignored Indonesia, Cambodia, and Laos. He did not mention Burma, Ceylon, and Nepal.

It is interesting that the Indonesians who had just rid themselves of a communist influence that seemed almost irreversible had urged that we pursue a policy of cessation of bombing as a prelude to a negotiated peace.

Some of the large questions:

What was the nature of the conflict? Was it a civil war, expanded? Perhaps a Chinese plot? Pure communist intrusion?

Where did the rest of Asia stand on this threat and how did they seem to interpret it?

Where did the Geneva Accords fit in? (Have you ever read this?) What about our World War II relationship to Ho Chi Minh and his followers?

All these were the phantom questions that a thinking, caring, religious community should voice in powerful outcry.

The End of American Innocence

Strangely, I don't know if it is more fruitful to discuss the sad history of our involvement in Vietnam, the enlargement of our Cold War concepts, our Chinese neurosis, or to begin simply with what the war did, not to the suburbs of Hanoi or the villages of the Mekong Delta, but to America.

For if anything has happened in the last several years, it is the final confirmation of the end of American innocence. Some people think that it began on that bleak (but sunny) afternoon in Dallas when an assassin shot the President of the United States (and school children clapped in Oklahoma).

But then we had lost Lincoln a century earlier and the American dream still pressed on to its higher atmosphere of hope and idealism.

But now, today, the violence touches our streets, so that ministers in Harlem carry revolvers when they step in and out of their own church buildings.

Social scientists have called it creative ferment. Wags called it "instant urban renewal." Newark, Rochester, Detroit, and Watts became living color in flames and disturbance.

It is apparent that we are going through more than just a national "adjustment," a single social revolution. It is urban, racial, an entire challenging of a system of values and goals.

If nothing else, Vietnam really has shown the ugly futility of war—modern or otherwise. It has made a farce out of the phony and misleading oratory that has been fed to the American people about "stopping communism" or "keeping our commitments." The healthiest and most hopeful result of this harrowing nightmare is a mood—rather, demand—by millions of people in America for a whole new vision of international affairs. A fresh and decisive analysis of this country's role in the world community. Peace is now a rallying word and the Christian community can make a stunning contribution to all of humanity if it can say the right words, with honesty and humility.

The writer of Hebrews, believed by many to be Paul, offers these words for consideration:

> Now may the God of peace who brought again from the dead our Lord Jesus, the great shepherd of the sheep, by the blood of the eternal covenant, equip you with everything good that you may do his will, working in you that which is pleasing in his sight. . . .

God, who was known and loved and worshiped and served, was the God of Peace!

From Old Testament to New, from Genesis to Revelation, the Holy One called the God of Peace reveals himself to man.

But the experience of peace, the use of the word, the interpretation of the experience are not always the same in scripture. If we are to probe the word's meaning and apply this powerfully to our lives, we should consider the shades of translation and usage.

The Elusive Gift

The fifteenth chapter of Genesis has the account of Abraham and his vision of God. And the Lord said to Abraham, "As for yourself, you shall go to your fathers in peace and you shall be buried in good old age." To be at peace meant a life after death that was full of serenity and assurance. It was God's gift to his servants and it spelled completeness and security.

We know the familiar expression for peace—*shalom*—as a greeting and salutation.

We also are aware of the larger use of this word to mean wholeness, health, completeness, and well-being.

Is this not what the Psalmist meant when he said:

> Pray for the peace of Jerusalem
> May they prosper who love you
> Peace be within your walls
> and security within your towers
> For my brethren and companions sake
> I will say, Peace be within you.

Peace was that experience of men and nation that was much more than the absence of warfare and strife—it was the sense of fulfillment in life that came from the covenant with God and one that extended through the hearts of the people.

Yet peace was as elusive then as it is now. Read through the accounts of the Old Testament and you find a nation constantly at war. Armies and maneuvers, and intrigue and battles, commanders, spies, equipment, and campaigns are more the standard of daily life in Israel than peace or concord or stability.

Could this be the reason that Isaiah's prophecy struck with such resounding force? Is this the background—the horror of continual conflict, masses of armies, crashing of drums and sabers and shields—that made the prophet's words cut so deeply in Israel's soul?

> For every boot of the tramping warrior in battle tumult and every garment rolled in blood will be burned as fuel for the fire.
>
> For to us a child is born, to us a son is given and the government will be upon his shoulder and his name shall be called Wonderful Counselor, Mighty God, Everlasting Father, Prince of Peace.

Now, that may well sound like Christmas but it wasn't offered in a yuletide context by Isaiah. He was looking over a national landscape that had been plowed with the bodies of young men from many nations.

He was searching, examining, and judging a national posture that drew most of its inspiration from the warrior and charioteer, the military procession, and the spoils of war.

But over the centuries this had turned sour—it was not enough to sustain the kingdom or comfort the widows or protect the orphans. Victors had a way of assuming godly powers and exerting moral judgments at the edge of the sword.

The spirit of the people was broken on the anvil of conflict or the axle of the chariot and the spike of the soldier.

Changing Patterns

Of all the writings of the Old Testament, is it strange that Jesus quotes Isaiah and Jeremiah more than any other—the two prophets so intent on changing the patterns of men's lives, the pretensions they coveted, and the false goals they sought.

Said Jeremiah, in the clear words of faith forged by a closeness to the eternal God:

> Let not the wise man glory in his wisdom
> let not the mighty man glory in his might
> let not the rich man glory in his riches
> but let him who glories, glory in this,
> that he understands and knows me,
> that I am the Lord who practices kindness,
> justice, and righteousness in the earth;
> for in these things I delight, says the Lord.

Now, the men and women of the New Testament used the word "peace" with the same fervor and depth that came from Old Testament origins—but some additional meanings were given.

One was the experience of peace and confidence in the world of turmoil and upheaval. Jesus said:

> Peace I leave with you, my peace I give unto you.

The Peace of God

I was riding in a taxicab in Washington, D.C., when the intensity of the war reached its full height in the Middle

East. I remarked to the cabdriver that we surely were living in time of struggle, war, and uncertainty. Here we were embroiled in a Vietnam war—now the fighting breaks out in the Holy Lands and Stokely Carmichael announces that the capital was in for a hot summer.

This did not phase him a bit. He said that his Christian faith had shown him how to be an island of peace in a sea of turbulence. In fact, the Bible, he said, predicted all of this—it was truth in action, all there to be read and understood. I came away with the feeling that he was slightly pleased at all the blood and rockets and insults and air strikes. He was a man of faith, surrounded by his spiritual armor that even the cries of this week's victims could not penetrate.

Yet before our ride and conversation were over, I discovered that my friend had been rightly interpreting not only a New Testament concept of peace, but also the personal experience of his life. He lives in the ghetto. He had struggled to find a meaning, purpose, dignity as a member of a tormented minority. In Jesus Christ he had found truly what the world could neither give nor take away—the peace of God. And it gave him joy and direction for the day ahead.

And so prominent it is throughout the writings of the New Testament—for here men and women struggled against the world, against the culture, at times, against family to be loyal to this new vision of God's love. They suffered so many losses we wonder that they stuck it out.

To have kept the faith may have been as basic as losing a job or breaking up a family or banishment from the neighborhood or imprisonment with the apostles or torture with the disciples. The peace of God—we call it a devotional phrase, but its practice was not won in church parlor readings or chapel discussions on piety. The peace of God was life in the face and midst of death.

And yet how ordinary and practical it could be in scripture, as well as encouragement to martyrs and saints. The peace of God was harmony in marriage, the source of domestic tranquility, the basis for household happiness.

It was also the foundation of the true amity and fellowship of the saints—for if they did not experience peace in the life of the church, where would it find a place to be expressed if not among Christ's own?

And so the priest turns to the faithful today and says:

> The Mass is over, go in peace, recalling the bond of reconciliation, love and unity with God the Father.

If we are tempted to conclude our understanding here, then we are reminded by Hebrews of something else:

> Now may the God of peace . . . working in you that which is pleasing in his sight . . .

The peace of God is meant to work through His servants as part of His creation. And that work is taken up in acts that would deny God's presence, it is to be implemented in every place where strife rules, war continues, conflict rides high, and the hot breath of hatred is confident and arrogant.

The peace of God is a cleansing, purging power that first is to take hold of us and then to be at work in the world, that God may be glorified and His Son honored.

The Fulfillment of Scripture

And if ever scripture is to be fulfilled it means reconciliation and peace along the Jordan, at the gate called Holy, in the sands of the Sinai desert, along the road to Damascus where troop carriers and half-tracks trace the steps of Paul.

Yet there is no regional peace unless you believe in a provincial God who rules Galilee but not the South China Sea, the One who judges Samaria but not Saigon, the Holy Other who nurtures his children in Haifa but not Hanoi.

This is a terrible time to claim Christian membership, for the world is asking us to own up. It's a day when the Prince of Peace is expected to have a few representatives on the stage of world opinion—to have some spokesmen speaking the word and telling it like it is. The God of Peace!

The Church and the Military

In the September 28, 1966, issue of the *Christian Century*, the feature "Pen-Ultimate" stated the problem for the institutional church and its supportive role of the military establishment in this country. Said the writers:

> We also know that some war-making will go on in the air and from the air, whence fall the bombs, missiles and napalm which splatter alike on just and unjust, combatant and noncombatant, man and woman, adult

and child, guilty and innocent. And we know that air war must be undertaken by people with needs which must be ministered unto. Hence chaplains, chapels and chapel windows.

Given all these awarenesses and partial justifications, we still wonder how much ideology has to fly with our bombers. Is not SAC protesting too much, bluffing a bit? Here is the rationale for the window:

Description of the Strategic Air Command Memorial Window

Text: *"Whom shall I send and who will go for us? . . . Here am I! Send me."* *Isaiah 6:8*

Most prominent in the design is the ray of golden light symbolic of God. His will, His revelation and His influence on the life of man. Standing in the fullness of God's will is man. He is responding to the challenge of God to serve his age—"Here am I! Send me." Mature in mind, and dedicated in spirit he stands upon the threshold of the unknown in response to the challenge of God, "Whom shall I send and who will go for us?" He is a servant of God and "Peace Is His Profession." Behind him is his family, symbolic of all the families he is dedicated to protect.

Around and above the man are the means given him by God to carry out his work. To the right are isobars, indicative of the weather services. Above are the planes he flies, one of which is being refueled during flight. The main flight of aircraft is bathed in a golden light similar to the rays of light descending from God, reminiscent of the motto "Peace Is Our Profession," and that this is the labor of God-fearing men. The mission calls for worldwide action. The outlines of a map of the world based on a north polar azimuthal equidistant projection, broken into four parts, are shown near the four corners of the window. Streaking across the window in an upward curve, is the path of power, inspired by the trail of a jet or rocket.

In the April 1968 edition of *The Chaplain,* Ormonde S. Brown reported on his studies of some two thousand airmen who had been recalled to duty during the Korean conflict.

These veterans had served in the Air Force in World War II and suddenly were reactivated into military service. Chaplain Brown, serving at Maxwell Air Force Base, was able to conduct an extensive survey—questionnaire of the attitudes and reactions of these returning servicemen. He was especially interested in the role of religion as it related to the motivation and character of this isolated group of two thousand servicemen. The recallees were personally processed and interviewed by the base chaplains.

Chaplain Brown gives the philosophy which motivated his article:

> Supersonic flying requires a special creation—pilots who have the courage to match its challenge, bodies to match its mysteries, minds to master its intricacies, and moral fiber to equal its demands on character. We need men who are well-nigh superhuman, god-like.
>
> Where do we get such men? We still get them from the wombs of our women. They are human, but they are that prematurely mature minority in whose hands resides our twilight destiny pending the advent of complete automation. They are not many. Perhaps they are neither too weak, nor too few. They are those amongst

us who are tried, tested, prepared in body and mind, true-blue. In their emergence and dedication lies our chief hope for physical survival.

Since character is at such a premium in the men who fly, what do we know concerning their moral, religious, and spiritual disposition or dynamic—the greatest single ingredient in these superlatively fine persons? Will this knowledge furnish a key to their behavior? And a further question: beginning with the configuration of known moral attitudes, how can we improve the product to assure reliable and moral responses?

Being a group of 2,000 mature citizens of good minds and good bodies we decided to ask each of them: How much do you think religion relates to combating Russian communism? One hundred and forty-two (142) didn't have any opinion on this question; but 1,325 believed religion helps combat it. An additional 510 men stated that religion is *the answer* to Russian communism. Only 51 of these 2,000 Americans thought religion irrelevant in combating communism.

Then Chaplain Brown offers this summary of his findings. Although he has not taken a survey since 1950, he feels that he can justify these conclusions, given the same servicemen, from the same geographic areas, with possibly the same religious affiliations:

How Do We Create the Men We Need?

Are these the men who fly our machines? Is it reasonable to suppose that for the same geographic area a similar sampling now would greatly differ? The obvious limitations of the survey have already been admitted—but what are some of the significant reflections of our study? Updated, we'll hazard a few guesses:

1. Only a few can qualify to fly today. These have placed upon them a terrific physical, moral, and mental burden.
2. A very large majority—nearly all—are believers in God, who seek to do his will, consider themselves his instruments.
3. Most of them clearly see the moral issues of our times and are prepared to take a stand for God and country. Even though they may gripe at length, they are prepared to make very considerable personal sacrifices if needed. (Good counseling helps at this point.)
4. There is a close correlation between preservice church and Sunday school training and the achievement of the desirable attributes of character.
5. There appears to be no other "common denominator" that even begins to parallel religious idealism in the total life of many. Most believe that religious faith is basic, existent, terrifically important, and the *only* ideology we have capable of matching and defeating communism.

How can we assure reliable moral responses in the Air Force pilots of tomorrow? Most of tomorrow's flyers are running around our bases today. They are the sons of those statistically described above. Primarily, they are our sons.

If it be true that religion furnishes the best type man—that "all men are religious"—why not deliberately, by precept and example, stimulate interest in chapel attendance, in building and furnishing chapel and religious education facilities of merit? More forthright support of those religious activities that create the product we must have is clearly indicated.

At the close he confidently observes:

> Persons spiritually controlled and restrained are imbued with the best possible discipline—a discipline emanating from within, requiring only direction from without.

What is alarming and most apprehensive to many within the Christian community is the manipulation and cultivation of religion for the "product" of war. This may be a legitimate function of religion—Rome and Greece and every other major culture have never been denied the support of their religious oracles. Ancient Israel is a fine example of the best blend possible between saber and salvation. I'm not sure that you can name a single government, king, dictator, president who was ever without religious support for any war or conflict.

But what is different today is what we claimed in the introduction. All these arrangements and agreements and alliances of the past—even past four or five years—are under searing attack and questioning and challenge. They are not sacred agreements any more. They are not immune from examination and/or debate. And the military as well as the ministry is going to feel the heat.

I think Harvey Cox brought this to the sharpest point. You may not like it or agree, but you cannot dodge it.

> To say that speaking of God must be political means that it must engage people at particular points, not

> just "in general." It must be a word about their own lives—their children, their job, their hopes and disappointments . . . a word which builds peace in a nuclear world, which contributes justice in an age stalked by hunger, which hastens the day of freedom in a society stifled by segregation.

And then a sentence which you can hang over the mantel of your hunting lodge:

> If the word is not a word which arises from a concrete involvement of the speaker in these realities, then it is not a Word of God at all but empty twaddle.

The New Frontier

It should be clear that the new frontier of the Christian community is going to be where the people are: at fun and play, at the computer center and the high-rise housing project. Yes, with the beautiful people who show the dogs and race the horses and hire the maids and the other beautiful people who are black and groom the horses and walk the dogs and are the maids.

We are in the last years of the church as we know it because we can never go back to the pleasant detached noon luncheons and afternoon teas and Wednesday-night prayer meetings and call this the mighty church of Christ. It may be some kind of church but it's not the one that is going to be in the cauldron of life, surrounded by the surging needs of humanity who are hungry for direction, depth, and hope.

We are in the last years of the church because instead

of ducking conflict and circling the bruises of life, the new saints will see every human encounter, event, experience as really filled with God's presence. God's presence may fill a moment of tender love, romance, or a period of forgiveness and reconciliation. God's presence may be felt in an outcry that foments an outburst for justice and recognition and is known in the pursuit of truth without censoring or tampering with or faking evidence.

But the new days of the Christian community are going to be scary and exhilarating because every situation counts and every person is a child of the Promise—whether they know it or like it or want it. And they may not be in the cathedral courtyard but a jailhouse prison yard. Sanctuaries are all about us and the Christian of these new years will be the opportunist who will enlarge the vision and expand the definitions that spell quality of life and wide-vision horizons.

I mean, isn't that what Easter was all about? Jesus was so great and God's power so atomic and love so unending that there is even room for colored eggs and nose-twitching rabbits and Fifth Avenue Charades and a busted family clothing account. Do Robert Hall's and Bond's and Lord and Taylor and J. C. Penney want to celebrate Easter? Well, why not? Jesus brought life, not death, expansion of the mind and spirit without LSD! If anybody's nervous about the whole new set of spiritual guidelines, it will probably be the church which nervously smiles at the millions who really would like to hear it for a change.

It can't all be processions and flowers and academic hoods. Thank goodness the Vatican lace has gone along with the white-calf slippers and hopefully in the not too distant future, the Swiss Guards. And the zombi gospel hymns and the fake language of faith. Perhaps we have just to flake off the scales to let the new hide emerge.

And this new adventure of faith is going to have its harrowing times of conflict and unexpected confusion. Life is so highly charged and so immediate now. The TV screen puts it right against your eyes and brain—but also into the depths of your heart.

Our Debt to Muhammad Ali

Every issue is there for the picking. The story of Cassius Clay is just about the best parable around for what I think will be the sharp, sudden events that require new understanding and new interpretation.

According to the last statement from the federal court in Texas, Clay owes the United States $10,000 and five years in prison. He was sentenced for refusing to take the oath of induction. While the conviction is being appealed, let us consider what we owe Cassius Clay.

First, the recognition that he is the best boxer around. He knocked the wrappings off everything in sight for seven years. Secular Sonny Liston and Believer Floyd Patterson still recall their last outing with the champ. His shadow will box every fighter who comes along. Pretenders will wonder if he ever really lost the title—no matter how many rounds they fight to claim it.

Second, we ought to be willing to call him by his chosen name—Muhammad Ali. As part of his Black Muslim religious experience, this new name is the one he wants. Is it so unfair to allow him this privilege and choice in free America? Or is it part of the defrocking ceremonies that after we take away his boxing title we shall also debase him by slurs over his name.

Third, at some point we might take seriously Muhammad Ali's extraordinary appeal and popularity among the Negro community. You may not like his credentials, his philosophy, or his most recent form of dissent—refusing induction. But surely we can admit his place of new leadership, whether or not it fits our brand of patriotism or piety. He has shown a willingness to take his medicine. Perhaps a larger question is—are we willing to take his criticism?

In many respects, Muhammad Ali looms much larger than his critics who own the sports palaces or the editorial pages. He has raised authentic questions about the war in Vietnam, politics and religion, and the rights of minorities in America. Boxing all of a sudden fades away with the appearance of these incendiary issues.

For a background, remember that the white community was pleased when Muhammad Ali was a good fighter—even with a "bad" religion. There was some disappointment that he didn't tap-dance or belt out Dixieland show tunes. Hard to picture him with watermelon or wheeling pink Cadillacs.

Their distress turned to alarm and then to fury when he made remarks about the war in Vietnam or the absence of Negroes on draft boards and juries.

At the height of this concern, Jimmy Brown, the all-time football star, hosted a quiet dinner in Cleveland for Muhammad Ali and a dozen top Negro sports stars. Bill Russell was there from Boston. Lew Alcindor winged in from California. Bobby Mitchell and Willie Davis and a few others sat in on the late-night session to challenge this young boxer and his unflinching dissent.

When it was all over, Brown told one sports writer, "He's extremely religious and with people like that religion comes first. What do you do with a man's belief? You leave it alone."

Unfortunately, we can't leave the Black Muslims alone. They bug us. They don't fit any theological pattern or system that is native American. Islam doesn't sound like Methodist or Presbyterian. They study Arabic, talk about Allah, and think Mecca. And their religion seems to be getting in the way of our wars.

Frankly, we may owe Muhammad Ali a thank-you note for defying our dreams and shattering our prejudices.

The Churches and Reconciliation

President Johnson once called for a National Day of Prayer for Reconciliation, August 7, 1967. He urged that religious leaders offer prayers for racial peace. I was struck with a certain dismay and apprehension. It seemed that instead of reaching out to the tragic needs of our urban society, we were beating a retreat into the sanctuary of religion, hoping that God would not forget us, although we regularly had failed him.

That may be a harsh judgment, but does our record support a more lenient criticism?

For the last two decades, the churches have been ignoring the ghetto and inner city. There are a few outposts of vigorous and lively witness, but generally the money and power and prestige has been invested in the slopes of suburbia. Whenever churchmen have rallied around the cause of racial justice, they have faced financial punishment from their own congregations.

In Rochester, New York, the Council of Churches supported Saul Alinsky's FIGHT organization, which had the original controversy with Eastman Kodak over jobs for Negroes. Although this yearlong agitation has finally been resolved, the Council of Churches lost $22,000 in contributions and faced an intolerable deficit.

In Cleveland, Ohio, several of the leading clergymen in the city were forced out of their pulpits because of outspoken stands on community racial problems.

Yes, the racial disorders of the American city should be a primary concern of all religious groups—a prayerful concern. But as the predominantly white community was called upon by a white President to pray for peace, I recalled that incident where the disciples sought to heal a very sick youngster. They failed and the desperate family turned to Jesus.

He healed the unfortunate victim, restoring his sanity and well-being. When the disciples asked why they were unable to overcome the evil spirit that was destroying the young man, Jesus replied, "This kind never comes out except by prayer and fasting." *Matthew 17:21*

Only by the total spiritual commitment of prayer, love, and intense faith would this evil spirit yield. The disciples had not, and most of us have not achieved such a single-minded devotion. Unfortunately, our Day of Reconciliation seemed like prayer by the whites and fasting for the Negroes.

Our family attended service at St. Peter's Lutheran Church in New York on the Sunday set aside by the President for prayer and reconciliation. I was startled, with many others, to hear the Epistle lesson for the day (selected a year in advance in liturgical churches) read from Luke 19:41–42.

> . . . And when he drew near and saw the city, he wept over it, saying, Would that even today you knew the things that make for peace!
>
> But they are hid from your eyes.

Christ Waits in the Ghetto

When the President called for the Day of Prayer, he also announced an eleven-man Special Advisory Commission on Civil Disorders. But I wonder if we really need another study to tell whitey to wake up! No more than we need another Senate hearing or a new church pronouncement. We have heard and studied and pronounced while rats roam and children cry and Detroit burns.

Whitney Young, Jr. isn't a preacher or the President, but he said it for both when he remarked:

> America has to decide whether it is going to exterminate or liberate the Negro.

We have had our day of prayer and reconciliation. This is in keeping with the example and teaching of Christ. Let us remember that He always followed prayer with action, that petitions became power, and people were changed in unusual and wonderful ways.

So let the bankers pray about finding new channels for mortgage and housing money, let the unions and employers startle us with new hope for jobs, let the educators and teachers initiate new programs, and let the churches stop running and start serving Christ in the ghetto. He is there waiting for them.

One of the best examples of how this can explode into new vistas of concern and outreach was described by the *Wall Street Journal:*

> One of the events that led Prudential Insurance Co. to help the Newark ghetto was a four-page letter, laboriously written to Orville Beal, president, by William Algernon Teal, a Negro youth.
>
> "The people, the houses and the environment are depressing," William then nineteen, wrote last summer. He explained that a household of six, including a grandmother, an aunt and three cousins, lived largely on the $210 a month his mother earned as an attendant at a mental hospital.
>
> "If I eat breakfast, it consists of grits and bread, and sometimes a piece of bacon," William wrote. "I hardly ever eat lunch. My dinner last night consisted of one hot dog, potato chips and a glass of water."
>
> But William had a bigger problem: He wasn't going to be able to continue at Shaw University, a Negro school in Raleigh, N.C., where he had completed two years. He hadn't been able to find a summer job. "Sir, my luck has run out!" the youth said. "I need 1,800 dollars to go back to college in September.
>
> "Sir, I beg of you if it is possible for you to give me a job in your personal employment. I will work as a

porter, dishwasher, floor cleaner, a personal valet, anything you can do will help."

William declared, "I do not uphold the riots, but I understand the reason for them. Sir, the white man has the power and therefore he must grant the justice. The only power the black man has is the power to disrupt."

"That one really got to us," a Prudential executive says. The company arranged a summer job for William, as a night porter, and got him a loan from one of the Newark banks so he could return to school.

«7»

The Remaining Years

Is it not time to ask if the present arrangement of things in the established church is the only way of fulfilling God's call to be a fellowship of believers? By arrangement I mean the setup for worship, the formalized (and often fossilized) manner of handling the sacraments. The stuffy, rigid, and predictable patterns of preaching. The very architecture of the stone church, the elevated bell tower, the row upon row of pews. The windows. The music of a kind performed by a choir of uncertain talents.

Perhaps the call for renewal in the church will take

care of all this. I doubt it. I think much of Protestantism is locked into the form described by Roger Hazelton:

> An overblown aestheticism has invaded affluent Protestantism, "enriching" services and "beautifying" churches. A "cathedral complex" has seized and victimized us. Earlier canons of sobriety and honesty have been violated right and left. God has been left without a witness. But religion has done well and prospered . . .

Earlier we talked about the flurry that is named the underground church. What is happening is that we have developed two specific types of churchmen, not unlike the great ocean liners that had two captains—one to sit at the banquets and invite the cruise members to share his table; the other to actually run the ship, issue the orders, and insure the safe arrival of the passengers and crew.

The concentration on the church as a place, a geographic location, is not enough to shape a powerful and meaningful witness to the world. Whether we search the scriptures or examine the exhortations of the saints for guidance, the body of Christ is primarily a fellowship called out of the world on one hand and, on the other, sent into the world to witness to the Name.

I don't believe it is possible for the church to be the leaven in the lump, the yeast in the bread and still maintain the "present arrangement of things." In fact, I challenge the arrangement of institutions, buildings, establishment centers as being competent to give a vigorous witness and critique of our contemporary world. The sheer numbers being generated by the population explosion alone tell us that the Christian community is no longer able to respond to this mass of people.

The church doesn't have the manpower and resources to approach its mission to the world in the "same old way." Even if it did, it should seriously be confronted with the results of its labor, an appraisal of its stewardship.

An obvious factor is the decline in the number of professional clergymen. Under the old strategy, there are no longer enough men and women in the ordination scene to take care of the communicants of the church. If this be true, who will reach out to the secular society, giving aid, assistance, and comfort to the people who are the children of God?

It is my conviction that we have entered the new day of the Christian faith. It is like no other time, for our resources and allies are extraordinary! Communication and technology are at every hand. Transportation is as close as a credit card. The mood of the secular community and the outsider is at times more responsive to the meaning of the gospel than is that of the certified Christians who have been officially notified!

Trends in the New Era

Let us indicate some of the trends in the new era of Christian expression.

1. The construction of church buildings, seminaries, schools should cease. There should be a moratorium on this type of building for at least ten years. Several reasons dictate this as a dynamic event. The American city is

loaded with empty and half-empty churches. Cities and towns have churches for sale. The rushing mood of optimism from the ecumenical discussions may release an amazing number of properties—the result of consolidation and merger. In city after city (and rural areas) there are thousands of natural and urgent mergers that should take place.

Furthermore, they should take place now, this year, not next year or in the sweet by and by. These churches and properties have become almost a curse upon the Christian community. An extravagant waste of time and energy and manpower to "keep them open." They are a sentence of despair to the dwindling congregation and almost a disease to the city or town that receives no aid on the tax rolls. A staggering amount of valuable land could be released for development and community betterment if such extensive mergers as I have described were to suddenly come about.

2. No new church properties should be constructed because we have really arrived at such an explosively different period in world urban history. The Church of the Middle Ages needed to be a massive fortress sort of layout to protect physically the weak and orphaned. It was often the only refuge against barbarian and vandal outrage. It was the resource for learning and art and scholarship. It was the household not only of faith, but of healing and help to the sick, the traveling, the pilgrim, and the dying. The church was total care—and assumed total concern all the way to the castle coronation and the exploration of new worlds.

People, this has all changed. Instead of the church

losing, it has won! The great universities of the world are hardly less concerned for learning or the advancement of theological studies than the church. The enormous public hospitals, the institutions of care and convalescence surely do not have to be church owned and operated to nourish the sick and comfort the dying. The trade unions and construction craftsmen surely do not have to be verified by the bishop or blessed by the monsignor. Police and fire and sanitation workers seem to function just as well with or without a communion breakfast. The press and publishing have maintained a much better standard of performance and quality when they are free from the nagging censorship of clericals or the threat of uncertain Inquisitions and Registers.

Praise God for Xerox

The church—its fellowship and witness is now free of so many housekeeping, vineyard-planting, scroll-copying chores. Praise God for Xerox! Praise the Creator for IBM, or does that not fit into your twentieth-century concept of Creation?

Do you see that God in his power and love has surrounded us with a dynamic, unfolding Creation that now calls forth the best and brightest gifts that the Christian gospel can afford? And those gifts are the enduring ones. The gracious word, the spontaneously good deed, the understanding moment, the enduring friendship. The marriage that has meaning and depth because it has integrity and eternity. The clear-eyed look at the world so that a word of judgment comes as swiftly as evil and wrong. And the sound of praise and support when the community or state or neighbor has touched a new plateau of excellence or achievement.

3. If all this be true or if at least some of the trends are starting to hum, then the layman will emerge as the man of this century. He will be prepared to devote a significant amount of his conscious effort for the Christian cause—away from church property.

4. Organized religion will depend more and more on the brainpower of the layman. The advance thinking and planning that must come forward will not wait on the musings of conservative clergymen or doddering bishops. Ideas, initiative, and adventure of the early church came from young people. Jesus was a young man and would have shocked most of the clergy today. Laymen need to be an uncontrolled force if the Christian fellowship is going to make it into the twenty-first century.

5. The new laymen will find their steady expression of Christian devotion with individuals and groups away from the church building. The location of his normal house of worship is too often a retreat center—like his home! Knowing this, he should expand his Christian awareness in all the vitality and ferment of his work and professional encounter. At the place of his employment, and even more, at the time and destinations of his travel!

6. The real story of the Christian impact will be told in the whirl and wonder of business. The government official, the business executive, the industrialists, the computer analysist all are caught up in the dynamics that shape and form the lives of urban society. The home has become saturated with the quiet pleasures of entertain-

ment, diversion, and rest. (Sure, I know about the family problems, the neighborhood tensions, the school squabbles, the congregational split. But that's for another time!) The church has been drawn into this setting and has an unfortunate secondhand connotation about it.

7. The real church comes for the man of faith when he decides to make this Christian commitment effective in the combat of his work. Here the Christian can be invisible and silent, or articulate and, at times, combative. The focus is no longer his faithfulness to Sunday ushering, his usual allotment of canvass calls, or his helping out with the family-night supper. Rather, it will be found in all the pain and progress of human relationships right on the job or wherever that job takes him. Many, of course, will not rise to this call. But those that do will give the church of Christian believers an entirely new presence in the world—that God loves and seeks.

8. Where will this scene be set? In the midst of human misery. The layman now has the energy, understanding, and single-minded devotion to seek it out. He no longer buys the option of church games, tuning chimes, or dusting pews. He refuses to insulate himself any more from the starkness of death, the stench of nursing homes, the terror of prisons, or the depression of mental institutions. He will either be alive or dead to his faith. No little in between. No buying his way in with a big pledge on the new cathedral. No shrugging off the theological questions to moral incompetents who dare to mention the words of Christ without ever intending to fulfill them. It will be a frightful, exhilarating period with very little ring-kissing

or candle-lighting—but then, neither did the disciples follow these exercises.

The New Laity and the Young Clergy

One of the natural and interesting alliances of the second half of the twentieth century will be the gathering of young pastors and the new laity. They meet across denominational lines, often not even in the same towns or neighborhoods. They come together on issues relating to the problems of humanity and finding fellowship "on the run." At present it is very unstructured and rather formless. But the groundwork—which is discussion, writing of papers, and conference discussion groups—will be the prepared soil of the next decade's harvest.

Gordon D. Gregg, an executive with IBM in Dayton, Ohio, turned away from the institutional church (where he had been a clergyman) to find his witness in the secular world.

His critique of the church—not unfriendly but surely incisive—is one that many young pastors and laymen would endorse. Said he:

> Almost all of our present structures are patterned after the military model from Roman times. Some have been modified more than others in an effort to decentralize power and authority after the model of our newer democratic forms. But basically our ecclesiastical institutions are still organized around a hierarchy or pyramid of power.
>
> This form of organization suited the church quite well

> so long as its primary functions were seen as the conservation and propagation of revealed truth and the conversion of the world through coercion—and so long as there was a coercible laity that was willing to play the role of Pfc's in the "Onward Christian Soldiers" army for the sake of salvation and a life after death.

How have the laymen reacted to this first-century world view of the church, theology, and the Christian life?

Concludes Gregg:

> Lucid and sophisticated laymen are finding the form of the institution to be dehumanizing and insulting and its first century world view anachronistic and naive if not down right stupid.

And the result of all this?

> . . . so long as the laity are forced to play the role of mindless sheep taking directions from their professional shepherds, the sheep that *have* minds of their own are going to jump the fence. And so long as the younger clergymen, who have been equipped with a theology adequate to a new age, are forced to operate under a reactionary and authoritarian hierarchy, they too will jump the fence.

A somewhat different approach brought Lynn Leavenworth to the same observation about the style of the emerging church and the mood of the young clergy and restless laity that make up its membership. When he studied the mood of seminaries and seminarians, Leavenworth concluded that:

> Secular motifs shift the attention away from the church organization as a major center for Christian ministry. Theologians, journalists, conferences, unceasingly drum into the mind that the self contained Christian organization as a major center for ministry is simply outdated. The church should go lose itself, because God acts in secular form.

Tomorrow Morning's Schedule

One example of the pioneer spirit working in the life of the Christian cause is Christ Church Presbyterian in Burlington, Vermont. In 1961 this gathering of believers decided that the last thing they needed was a half-million-dollar building gracing another New England green. No yearning for colonial towers or white picket fences. Forget the hurricane lamps and Indian shutters on the parish house. This collection of innovators put down their intention on paper by saying:

> We believe it to be the primary job of the church to seek where God is at work and to follow him there in obedient service. We believe that God is at work in Burlington . . . in our homes, our places of work, our jail, our city hall, our slums, our playground, our schools and our churches.

They enlarged on this definition as their imaginative schedules took in the political, social, and educational needs of their city and state. They found an old radio-

TV repair shop, next door to a former boat showroom, and turned it into a meeting place. Folding chairs and coffee cups and screw-in lights were just fine as a start. The world was the center of action. The community of believers set out on a very nontraditional course for a New England parish. Can this be the shape of the future, as the people of Christ begin to improvise their witness and worship?

I believe that the biggest step forward in the new life of the Christian cause comes when we break away from the buildings and grounds. We can relax on the space problem, the house of worship worries, when our interests are in soul brothers!

Tomorrow Morning's Space

If we cut down on the building and increase the output of our wordly mission, the space problem will be solved in many possible ways. Schools, public and private, can be used or rented without any extra church and state tension. Private homes worked rather well in the first three centuries and even some of today's spreads have a cathedral living room!

There are vast and almost unnumbered institutions that have meeting rooms and assembly halls. They are the fraternal and sorority organizations. Think of the space on college and university campuses. Even suburban banks and utility companies make available public rooms for the community.

If we really want to move out into the sphere of larger encounter, we can avail ourselves of the public halls.

There are twelve thousand motion-picture theaters in the United States—how many of these are possible for Sunday morning rental at a low cost? There are six thousand drive-in theaters—with every day until evening available, with parking!

It would appear that our obsession with our "own house of worship" has become so compulsive that it borders on the neurotic. The early Christians, under persecution and public pressure, met in the catacombs under Rome. There must be a hundred thousand funeral homes that would be open to Christian groups that needed space for discussion, worship, and planning. Think of the effect this would have on funeral practices!

And go outdoors. Last Easter a group of youngsters under the care of the Christian Herald Association held their own sunrise service in Central Park. After the early program outdoors, the young people went to a nearby Horn and Hardart cafeteria for breakfast and a discussion of "What Easter Means to Me." Space and location are no longer problems. We want to be with people, not property.

Tomorrow Morning and Tomorrow Night

The perceptive, eager Christian is going to pursue his calling in the world about him. His energy is no longer needed in worry over the basic provisions of life. His concern is to see that people are taken care of and he will offer his best assistance in *crisis situations.*

People by the millions are in distress and trouble and in need of a Savior. They are often in upheaval during a job change, a house hunting, in school registration, in college entrance. Young people are on the brink of moral quicksand when they enter the university, depart for the army, take a vacation in Europe, or move to the city.

Older people are distraught and frightened by the terrifying power of the city and their sense of loneliness and separateness in a culture that praises youth and curses age.

The avant garde of the Christian community must see its fulfilling purpose in the employment bureaus, the casting agencies, the divorce courts, and prisons. In all the waiting rooms of life. Into the prisons and hospitals and nursing homes. Into the sanitariums where people hunger for an intelligent and thoughtful voice.

Some of our church people feel especially proud of Dial-a-Prayer. Yet we need the manpower to take this to its natural and proper effect: real people answering the immediate questions and concerns and cries of individuals in trouble and need. Every urban center should have a battery of competent lay people answering phones and responding to the struggle for meaning and life—live! Think what this can mean in a city like Chicago or New York where a stranger, a girl in trouble, an elderly woman facing eviction could turn to strong and immediate assistance from caring, vital people. The difference is that between hope and despair, between life and death.

This advertisement appeared in the New York *Times:*

Doctors' Shangri-La

Why struggle? Avoid big-city case overloads; early burnout.

> Enjoy all the advantages of small town living in a modern, progressive community, convenient to, but safely distant from, big-city hospital and cultural facilities.
>
> Relaxed golfing, boating, fishing, hunting and winter sports five minutes from home or hospital. Opportunity exists for a staff surgeon and one or more general practioners in a populous area served by a modern, fully equipped general hospital that has just completed a million dollar expansion. For full particulars, write X 7462 TIMES

Some people would substitute the word clergy for doctor to describe the mood of the profession and the church! But no more. When Dietrich Bonhoeffer pondered this question of bewildered and wandering humanity he wrote to a friend in 1931:

> to this hopeless, suffering mankind, Jesus Christ, the great hope, is preached!

There are sermons that need to be preached in the lives of those who believe this Man. There is no special oratory required. It is done without notes or manuscript. It comes from the heart to another heart.

If Jesus Returned Today

Just what did William Faulkner mean but that the Christian people had fallen short when one of his characters in *The Wild Palms* was to say:

> If Jesus returned today we would have to crucify him in our own defense to justify and preserve the

civilization we have worked and suffered and died for two thousand years to create and perfect in man's own image.

Too strong? Overstated? Might we ask, after a reading of Ezekiel 34, just what the primary thrust of the church should be? Is it to bolster the status quo, enforce the dominant social values, maintain a silent vigil at the pretensions of power? Not in the Bible.

Not in the biblical sense of justice, the struggle for truth, the allegiance to a God who would be known and served in the activities of men.

Let's take a quick reading of Ezekiel 34:

> Therefore, you shepherds, hear the word of the Lord: As I live, says the Lord God, because my sheep have become a prey, and my sheep have become food for all the wild beasts, since there was no shepherd; and because my shepherds have not searched for my sheep, but the shepherds have fed themselves, and have not fed my sheep; therefore, you shepherds, hear the word of the Lord: Thus says the Lord God, Behold, I am against the shepherds; and I will require my sheep at their hand, and put a stop to their feeding the sheep; no longer shall the shepherds feed themselves. I will rescue my sheep from their mouths, that they may not be food for them.
>
> For thus says the Lord God: Behold, I, myself will search for my sheep, and will seek them out. As a shepherd seeks out his flock when some of his sheep have been scattered abroad, so will I seek out my sheep; and I will rescue them from all places where they have been scattered on a day of clouds and thick darkness.